Verbal Reasoning

10 Minute Tests

9–10 years

TEST 1: Similars and Opposites

Underline the two words in each line which are most similar in type or meaning.

Example	<u>dear</u>	pleasant	poor	extravagant	<u>expensive</u>
1	flexible	rigid	stiff	friendly	clever
2	table	mirror	basin	door	bath
3	apple	pear	carrot	rose	nettle
4	busy	clear	stormy	quick	obvious
5	lorry	aeroplane	boat	yacht	train

Underline the two words, one from each group, which are the most opposite in meaning.

Example	(dawn, <u>early</u>, wake)	(<u>late</u>, stop, sunrise)
6	(tidy, burn, flame)	(neat, messy, fire)
7	(house, soft, concrete)	(hard, cement, stable)
8	(right, river, solid)	(liquid, rigid, water)
9	(confident, timid, bashful)	(careful, tearful, shy)
10	(high, over, beside)	(through, under, above)

Underline the pair of words most similar in meaning.

Example	come, go	<u>roam, wander</u>	fear, fare
11	half, crumb	complete, whole	right, wrong
12	grip, clasp	release, hold	balance, fall
13	answer, question	repair, spoil	problem, difficulty
14	appear, arrive	come, go	disappear, return
15	warm, cool	climb, drop	feel, touch

Underline the word in brackets that is most opposite in meaning to the word in capitals.

Example	WIDE	(broad	vague	long	<u>narrow</u>	motorway)
16	GIVE	(present	grant	result	spare	take)
17	FLAT	(house	even	odd	bumpy	high)
18	BELOW	(under	above	on	beneath	between)
19	SHINY	(dull	quick	cloud	metal	sum)
20	END	(corner	side	beginning	middle	top)

TEST 2: Sorting Words 1

Test time: 0 – 5 – 10 minutes

Underline the one word in the brackets which will go equally well with both the pairs of words outside the brackets.

Example rush, attack   cost, fee   (price, hasten, strike, <u>charge</u>, money)

1. leave, separate   piece, share   (bit, portion, part, holiday, section)
2. beat, punch   success, achievement   (hit, smack, purpose, thump, give)
3. box, case   stem, torso   (tree, trunk, luggage, suitcase, body)
4. shiny, glowing   clever, intelligent   (dull, light, bright, smart, quick)
5. dig, sow   tree, bush   (leaf, vegetable, spade, rake, plant)

Underline the two words which are the odd ones out in the following groups of words.

Example black   <u>king</u>   purple   green   <u>house</u>

6. shirt   vest   socks   shoes   trousers
7. ferry   bicycle   yacht   skateboard   windsurfer
8. eyes   hat   nose   mouth   glove
9. middle   edge   bottom   border   side
10. safe   secure   sausage   sound   sick

Rearrange the muddled letters in capitals to make a proper word. The answer will complete the sentence sensibly.

Example A BEZAR is an animal with stripes.   ZEBRA

11. Two TNNIOCNTES of the world are Africa and Asia.   _____
12. The storm brought down an ECLETRCI cable.   _____
13. Don't forget to lock the RTOFN door!   _____
14. We are going to the ASEDIES on Saturday if it is sunny.   _____
15. Sarah loves ice cream with COHCOTELA sauce.   _____

Find and underline the two words which need to change places for the sentence to make sense.

Example She went to <u>letter</u> the <u>write</u>.

16. Dairy give us cows products.
17. Number other is on the twenty side of the street.
18. Some were given you homework.
19. Can you close door the please?
20. My red is blue and shirt.

Total

Test 3: Sorting Words 2

Test time: 0 — 5 — 10 minutes

Add one letter to the word in capital letters to make a new word. The meaning of the new word is given in the clue.

Example	PLAN	simple	_plain_
1	HAIR	seat	_____
2	SPED	pay out	_____
3	ROOF	evidence	_____
4	SALLOW	not deep	_____
5	HEEL	car part	_____

Find a word that is similar in meaning to the word in capital letters and that rhymes with the second word.

Example	CABLE	tyre	_wire_
6	FOOTWEAR	two	_____
7	MASTER	sword	_____
8	NARRATE	smell	_____
9	MOULDY	mail	_____
10	SHATTER	take	_____

Underline the two words that are made from the same letters.

Example	TAP	PET	<u>TEA</u>	POT	<u>EAT</u>
11	DANCE	LANCE	LANES	CRANE	CLEAN
12	SLOPE	POLES	POSTS	LEAPS	PEEPS
13	FLAIR	FIRES	RIFLE	FRAIL	ROOFS
14	SWIRL	LOWER	WINGS	SWING	GRINS
15	LEAST	LASTS	STOOL	SLIPS	TALES

Rearrange the letters in capitals to make another word. The new word has something to do with the first two words.

Example	spot	soil	SAINT	_STAIN_
16	chair	bench	TEAS	_____
17	bound	jump	PALE	_____
18	cord	string	PORE	_____
19	fall	drip	PROD	_____
20	instruct	train	CHEAT	_____

4

Total

Test 4: Selecting Words

Underline two words, one from each group, that go together to form a new word. The word in the first group always comes first.

Example (hand, <u>green</u>, for)   (light, <u>house</u>, sure)

1. (hand, foot, way)   (signal, path, shoe)
2. (green, apple, wood)   (picker, leaf, land)
3. (straw, hay, pink)   (berry, cloud, stick)
4. (old, bald, handy)   (horse, tyre, man)
5. (white, blue, clean)   (bath, wash, sky)

Find the letter which will end the first word and start the second word.

Example peac (h) ome

6. pla (___) ard
7. thin (___) ing
8. blu (___) yes
9. fou (___) eal
10. flo (___) ind

Complete the following sentences by selecting the most sensible word from each group of words given in the brackets. Underline the word selected.

Example The (<u>children</u>, boxes, foxes) carried) the (houses, <u>books</u>, steps) home from the (greengrocer, <u>library</u>).

11. Michael picked up the (oars, rubbish, pigeon) and expertly (climbed, talked, rowed) the boat to the (castle, shore, school).
12. The (rocket, train, promise) blasted into the (sky, rails, room) from the space (station, town, letter).
13. Mrs Patel (dropped, carried, drove) her car (under, into, between) the parking space and (sped, cleaned, turned) off the engine.
14. My (uncle, aunt, dog) Trevor is my (pet's, mother's, desk's) (chair, brother, wall).
15. Mr Bowen bent (up, down, along) to smell the (fragrant, cold, easy) rose in his (garden, bathroom, cupboard).

Underline the one word which **cannot** be made from the letters of the word in capital letters.

	Example	STATIONERY	stone	tyres	ration	<u>nation</u>	noisy
16		RAINSTORM	stain	month	train	mains	roast
17		FAVOURABLE	blare	flour	brave	flavour	bluff
18		MARGARINE	argue	grain	margin	grime	enigma
19		HINDQUARTERS	quart	trend	strand	quince	trade
20		CRISPBREAD	price	pears	brisk	drape	pride

Test 5: Finding Words

Find the four-letter word hidden at the end of one word and the beginning of the next word. The order of the letters may not be changed.

Example The children had bats and balls. _____sand_____

1. Please wait for me. _____
2. Your football team is good this season. _____
3. Jane painted her room peach and cream. _____
4. I need to remember to lock the front door. _____
5. Please stick the label to your jacket. _____

Find the three-letter word which can be added to the letters in capitals to make a new word. The new word will complete the sentence sensibly.

Example The cat sprang onto the MO. _____USE_____

6. She has grown her H long. _____
7. We went to France for our HOLI. _____
8. The village shop S at six o'clock yesterday. _____
9. The ambulance RUD the sick person to hospital. _____
10. Every morning Luke eats a B of cereal. _____

Find a word that can be put in front of each of the following words to make new, compound words.

Example cast   fall   ward   pour   _____down_____

11	berry	board	currant	bird	_____
12	cuff	bag	rail	shake	_____
13	pot	spoon	cake	time	_____
14	stairs	stream	standing	roar	_____
15	boat	buoy	span	less	_____

Move one letter from the first word and add it to the second word to make two new words.

Example hunt   sip   _____hut_____   _____snip_____

16	fair	way	_____	_____
17	march	cob	_____	_____
18	every	early	_____	_____
19	teach	flee	_____	_____
20	climb	path	_____	_____

TEST 6: Alphabetical Order and Substitution

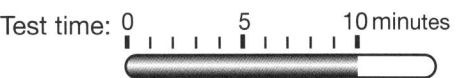

Underline the word in each line that has its letters in alphabetical order.

1	flare	flour	floor	fable	feeds
2	hosts	hilly	hello	hares	hinge
3	apply	above	acorn	adept	after
4	badger	better	believe	begging	begins
5	dwell	dizzy	defrost	deity	dense

If these words were written backwards and then placed in alphabetical order, which word would come fifth? Underline your answer.

6	ladle	paddle	little	stile	female
7	garland	garage	gallant	galaxy	gadget
8	goodness	fairness	kindness	sadness	likeness
9	biscuit	racket	ticket	chariot	bucket
10	nears	bears	fears	rears	tears

If A = 13, B = 10, C = 8, D = 6 and E = 1, find the answers to the following calculations.

11 A – E = _____
12 BD = _____
13 (B – C) + D = _____
14 C + D + E = _____
15 (A – C) + D = _____

If A = 2, B = 3, C = 5, D = 6 and E = 10, give the answer to each of these calculations as a letter.

16 E – C = _____
17 B + A + C = _____
18 D ÷ A = _____
19 E – (B + C) = _____
20 A × B = _____

TEST 7: Word Progressions

Test time: 0 — 5 — 10 minutes

Look at the first group of three words. The word in the middle has been made from the other two words. Complete the second group of three words in the same way, making a new word in the middle.

Example   PAIN   INTO   TOOK   ALSO   __SOON__   ONLY

1	FEES	SINK	INKY	POST	_____	REEK
2	DEAR	ARCH	CHIP	MOST	_____	ARMY
3	BOAT	OATS	PINS	PEAS	_____	GOAT
4	GEAR	GOLF	WOLF	CROW	_____	SLAM
5	PART	PANE	WINE	EXAM	_____	KNIT

Change the first word into the last word, by changing one letter at a time and making a new, different word in the middle.

Example   CASE   __CASH__   LASH

6	BIRD	_____	WIND
7	TASK	_____	WALK
8	BELT	_____	BALL
9	WING	_____	SONG
10	FAME	_____	FARM

Change the first word of the third pair in the same way as the other pairs to give a new word.

Example   bind, hind   bare, hare   but, __hut__

11	take, teak	mate, meat	sale, _____
12	list, silt	last, salt	left, _____
13	fate, rate	fake, rake	fail, _____
14	wind, find	wool, fool	wall, _____
15	tops, spot	leer, reel	keep, _____

Find the missing number by using the two numbers outside the brackets in the same way as the other sets of numbers.

Example   2 [8] 4   3 [18] 6   5 [25] 5

16	7 [15] 8	6 [9] 3	13 [__] 3
17	2 [1] 2	4 [2] 2	6 [__] 3
18	4 [8] 2	4 [12] 3	3 [__] 5
19	13 [2] 11	21 [9] 12	16 [__] 8
20	3 [9] 3	8 [16] 2	5 [__] 4

TEST 8: Logic

Read the statements and then underline two of the five options below that must be true.

1–2 'Some roofs are made of tiles. All houses have roofs.'

All roofs are made of tiles. All houses have tiles.
Tiles are a type of roof covering. Straw can be a roof covering.
A house needs a roof.

3–4 'The police help to keep us safe and catch criminals. Some police officers wear helmets.'

Police officers must wear helmets at all times. Police officers often work in pairs.
Helmets may be part of a police officer's uniform. People feel safer when there is less crime.
Police officers help to catch people who break the law.

In a pet shop there are 5 hutches in a row. A different rabbit is in each hutch. Work out, from the clues, where each rabbit belongs.

1	2	3	4	5

The black rabbit is next to the white rabbit with red eyes.
The floppy eared rabbit is in one of the end hutches.
The fat rabbit is not next to the brown and white rabbit, and it is further to the right than the floppy eared rabbit.
The brown and white rabbit is between the floppy eared rabbit and the white rabbit.

5–9 HUTCH 1 _____ HUTCH 3 _____ HUTCH 5 _____
HUTCH 2 _____ HUTCH 4 _____

Sam and Otis play football. Bob, Mike and Ravi play football and cricket.
Tom, Mike and Sam play rugby. Everyone likes computer games except Ravi.

10 Who likes cricket and rugby? _____
11 How many children like computer games? _____
12 Who likes rugby but not football? _____
13 How many children like football but not computer games? _____
14 Who likes football and rugby but not cricket? _____

Janet's bookshelves are divided into 6 areas. She keeps different items in each section. From the information below, work out what goes into each section.

A	B
C	D
E	F

The novels are directly above the reference books.
The novels are directly to the right of the CDs.
The photographs are directly to the left of the DVDs.
The DVDs are above the novels.
The CDs are higher than the school books but lower than the photos.

15–20 novels ____ reference books ____ CDs ____
school books ____ photographs ____ DVDs ____

Time for a break! Go to Puzzle Page 42

Total

TEST 9: Codes

Here are the number codes for four words. Match the right code to the right word.

BEND   BIND   BOOK   KIND
6538   0138   6138   6440

1 BEND _____   2 BIND _____
3 BOOK _____   4 KIND _____
5 Using the same code, decode 8435. _____

Solve the problems by working out the codes.

6   If 7914 is the code for FOUR, what does 794 stand for? _____
7   If 5612 is the code for MACE, what does 1652 stand for? _____
8   If 9461 is the code for PORE, what does 6491 stand for? _____
9   If 4813 is the code for CART, what does 183 stand for? _____
10 If 6972 is the code for TAME, what does 726 stand for? _____

Solve the problems by working out the letter codes. The alphabet has been written out to help you.

A B C D E F G H I J K L M N O P Q R S T U V W X Y Z

Example   In a code, SECOND is written as UGEQPF.
How would you write THIRD?   __VJKTF__

11 In a code, BISCUIT is written as CJTDVJU. How would you write BITS? _____
12 In a code, STEAM is written as UVGCO. How would you write MAST? _____
13 In a code, BRING is written as CSJOH. How would you write BEEN? _____
14 In a code, WHITE is written as VGHSD. How would you write HEEL? _____
15 In a code, PRIME is written as NPGKC. How would you write FOUL? _____
16 In a code, DREAM is written as GUHDP. Decode PDGH. _____
17 In a code, BRAIN is written as FVEMR. Decode RIIH. _____
18 In a code, GRIME is written as FQHLD. Decode FDQL. _____
19 In a code, FLOUR is written as DJMSP. Decode BCCN. _____
20 In a code, DRESS is written as CQDRR. Decode AHSD. _____

Test 10: Sequences

Test time: 0 — 5 — 10 minutes

Choose two words, one from each set of brackets, to complete the sentence in the best way.

Example   Smile is to happiness as (drink, <u>tear</u>, shout) is to (whisper, laugh, <u>sorrow</u>).

1   River is to water as (stream, vein, fridge) is to (cold, blood, kitchen).
2   Winter is to cold as (summer, spring, fire) is to (log, hot, sunshine).

Complete the following sentence in the best way by choosing one word from each set of brackets.

Example   Tall is to (tree, <u>short</u>, colour) as narrow is to (thin, white, <u>wide</u>).

3   Fish is to (fingers, pond, gills) as man is to (car, lungs, dinner).
4   Begin is to (finish, start, continue) as end is to (rear, finish, bottom).
5   Pause is to (break, snap, claws) as halt is to (go, start, stop).

Fill in the missing letters and numbers. The alphabet has been written out to help you.
A B C D E F G H I J K L M N O P Q R S T U V W X Y Z

Example   AB is to CD as PQ is to <u>RS</u>.

6   ZX is to YW as XV is to ____.
7   Ae is to Fj as Ko is to ____.
8   ST is to UV as WX is to ____.
9   P3 is to O5 as N7 is to ____.
10 HJ is to JL as LN is to ____.

Give the missing numbers and letters in the following sequences.

Example   2   4   6   8   10   <u>12</u>

11   24   20   16   12   8   ____
12   6   7   9   ____ 16   21
13   5   ____ 13   17   21   25
14   101   202   ____ 404   505   606
15   15t   17t   19u   21u   ____ 25v

Give the missing letters in the following sequences.
The alphabet has been written out to help you.
A B C D E F G H I J K L M N O P Q R S T U V W X Y Z

Example   CQ   DP   EQ   FP   GQ   <u>HP</u>

16   EK   GL   ____ KN   MO   OP
17   MN   ____ OR   PT   QV   RX
18   PQ   PR   ____ QT   RU   RV
19   PZ   QX   PV   QT   PR   ____
20   Gu   ____ Is   Jr   Kq   Lp

Test 11: Mixed

Test time: 0 — 5 — 10 minutes

Rearrange the muddled letters in capitals to make a proper word. The answer will complete the sentence sensibly.

Example A BEZAR is an animal with stripes. __ZEBRA__

1. If I make mistakes with my pencil, I use my BURREB. _____
2. At the beach I play with my TECKUB and spade. _____
3. In AUJANYR the weather is likely to be cold. _____
4. A bee or wasp GNIST is painful. _____
5. If you light matches near petrol there will be an ELXOPSOIN. _____
6. At RITCHSMAS we sing carols. _____

Answer these questions. The alphabet has been written out to help you.

A B C D E F G H I J K L M N O P Q R S T U V W X Y Z

7. Put the letters in the word SPECIAL in alphabetical order. _____
8. Which is now the fifth letter? _____
9. Put the letters in the word PREACH in alphabetical order. _____
10. Which is now the fourth letter? _____

Find a word that is similar in meaning to the word in capital letters and that rhymes with the second word.

Example CABLE   tyre   __wire__

11. MARK   mane   _____
12. TERROR   deer   _____
13. SHOP   moor   _____
14. PRESERVE   wave   _____
15. WICKED   while   _____

Solve the problems by working out the codes.

16. If the code for FLAMES is SDQRPN, what is the code for SEAM? _____
17. If the code for BLAST is XNRFE, what is the code for STALL? _____
18. If the code for QUITE is 59432, what is the code for TIE? _____
19. If the code for TWIST is bxyzb, what is the code for SIT? _____
20. If the code for SLUMP is FTRXY, what is the code for PLUM? _____

TEST 12: Mixed

If these words were listed in reverse alphabetical order, which word would come second? The alphabet has been written out to help you.

A B C D E F G H I J K L M N O P Q R S T U V W X Y Z

1. brooch   break   bracken   bruise   bridge   _____
2. chimney   choose   cherub   cheek   chapel   _____
3. penguin   pedal   penny   peony   pecan   _____
4. darkness danger   dancing   dampen   dainty   _____

Solve the problems by working out the codes.

5. If 8641 is the code for TEAS, what does 1648 stand for? _____
6. If 3996 is the code for GOOD, what does 693 stand for? _____
7. If 6752 is the code for MITE, what does 5762 stand for? _____
8. If 8491 stands for GRAB, what does 194 stand for? _____

Complete the following expressions by filling in the missing word.

Example   Pen is to ink as brush is to ___paint___.

9. Kennel is to dog as stable is to _____.
10. Cushion is to chair as pillow is to _____.
11. Butterfly is to six legs as bird is to _____ legs.
12. Picture is to wall as rug is to _____.

Town A is directly north of Town B.
Town C is west of B but south of D.
If the towns make a square on a map, where is

13. D in relation to A? _____   14. A in relation to C? _____
15. D in relation to B? _____   16. B in relation to D? _____

If A = 24, B = 12, C = 8, D = 4 and E = 2, give the answer to these calculations as a letter.

17. A ÷ B = _____   18. B + C + D = _____
19. (B − C) + D = _____   20. $\dfrac{DE}{E}$ = _____

Test 13: Mixed

Find the three-letter word which can be added to the letters in capitals to make a new word. The new word will complete the sentence sensibly.

Example The cat sprang onto the MO. ___USE___

1 The queen does not often wear a CN. _____
2 Nadia laid the table with four knives and KS. _____
3 That grocery S is more expensive than the one we use. _____
4 WE you knocked your head, you have a bruise. _____
5 The PR went out so we sat by candlelight all night. _____

Which one letter can be added to the front of all these words to make new words?

Example _c_ are   _c_ at   _c_ rate   _c_ all

6 ___ ass   ___ ink   ___ ray   ___ at
7 ___ how   ___ at   ___ even   ___ and
8 ___ our   ___ oal   ___ ox   ___ ear
9 ___ pen   ___ range ___ at   ___ men

Fill in the missing letters and numbers. The alphabet has been written out to help you.

A B C D E F G H I J K L M N O P Q R S T U V W X Y Z

Example AB is to CD as PQ is to _RS_.

10 GH is to KL as OP is to ____.
11 DF is to HJ as LN is to ____.
12 M8 is to L9 as K10 is to ____.
13 Mn is to Qr as Uv is to ____.
14 ZX is to VT as RP is to ____.
15 ST is to QR as OP is to ____.

Underline the word in the brackets closest in meaning to the word in capitals.

Example UNHAPPY (unkind death laughter <u>sad</u> friendly)

16 TRAIL   (measure ward   pass   home   path)
17 HONOUR   (obey   lord   praise   order   hot)
18 PETROL   (oil   car   garage   engine   fuel)
19 DISCOVER (hide   treasure misplace find   purchase)
20 CRIMSON   (blue   red   paint   flower   sky)

14

Test 14: Mixed

Underline the two words, one from each group, which are closest in meaning.

Example (race, shop, <u>start</u>) (finish, <u>begin</u>, end)

1 (conceal, jelly, carnival) (show, mask, mould)
2 (danger, past, menace) (threaten, safety, annoy)
3 (orange, skin, huge) (body, colour, peel)
4 (tape, tune, melon) (melody, worm, violin)
5 (excited, happy, miserable) (smile, cry, sad)

Here are some symbol codes for four words. Match the right codes to the right words.

BOOT	BROW	TRAY	WARY
? Q + =	X 5 5 ?	£ + Q =	X Q 5 £

6 BOOT _____
7 BROW _____
8 TRAY _____
9 WARY _____

Using the same code, decode:

10 £ + Q ? _____
11 Q 5 5 ? _____

Give the missing numbers and letters in the following sequences.

Example 5 21 8 17 11 13 <u>14</u> 9

12 4   ___ 6   6   8   9   10 12
13 Q8 B5 Q10 B6 Q12 B7 ___ B8
14 a17 a4 ___ b5 c13 c6 d11 d7
15 42 F 35 H ___ J 21 L
16 3   5   6   ___ 9   9   12 11

If P = 2, Q = 3, R = 4, S = 14 and T = 15, find the answer to the following calculations.

17 $\frac{S}{P} + Q =$ _____

18 $S - QR =$ _____

19 $\frac{T}{Q} + R =$ _____

20 $S + PQ =$ _____

15

TEST 15: Mixed

Add one letter to the word in capital letters to make a new word. The meaning of the new word is given in the clue.

Example PLAN simple __plain__

1 FEED released _____
2 FIST before second _____
3 LENT sloped _____
4 EAVES departs _____

Solve the problems by working out the letter codes. The alphabet has been written out to help you.

A B C D E F G H I J K L M N O P Q R S T U V W X Y Z

Example In a code, SECOND is written as UGEQPF. How would you write THIRD? __VJKTF__

5 In a code, READY is written as SFBEZ. What is YARD? _____
6 In a code, BARKS is written as DCTMU. What is WIND? _____
7 In a code, TOKEN is written as RMICL. What is SOCK? _____
8 In a code, CRESS is written as BQDRR. What is BEST? _____
9 In a code, HOUSE is written as FMSQC. What is SHOE? _____
10 In a code, FARMS is written as HCTOU. What is FAIL? _____

Change the first word of the third pair in the same way as the other pairs to give a new word.

Example bind, hind   bare, hare   but, __hut__

11 bore, robe   dome, mode   file, _____
12 rail, bail   rush, bush   rook, _____
13 fare, fear   lane, lean   lake, _____
14 town, down   tusk, dusk   trip, _____
15 tale, late   lose, sole   newt, _____
16 doom, mood   draw, ward   flow, _____

If A = 15, B = 12, C = 8, D = 3 and E = 1, find the answer to the following calculations.

17 A − C = _____
18 (B + C) − E = _____
19 $\frac{A}{D} =$ _____
20 (B − C) + D = _____

TEST 16: Mixed

Underline the one word which cannot be made from the letters of the word in capital letters.

Example   STATIONERY   stone   tyres   ration   <u>nation</u>   noisy

1	GABERDINE	greed	engine	bread	drain	bride
2	DASTARDLY	tardy	yards	saddle	darts	astral
3	APOLOGISE	goals	spool	pages	igloo	police
4	NEWSPAPER	wasps	spear	prawns	spare	preen
5	APPARATUS	strap	sprat	parts	arrest	traps

Find the four-letter word hidden at the end of one word and the beginning of the next word. The order of the letters may not be changed.

Example   The children had bat<u>s and</u> balls.   _____sand_____

6   Mum buys fruit at the market.   _____
7   That is my best arrangement today.   _____
8   I will brush my teeth another time.   _____
9   Half the class wandered in late.   _____
10 Must I brush under the desks too?   _____

Move one letter from the first word and add it to the second word to make two new words.

Example   hunt   sip   _____hut_____   _____snip_____

11   play   sap   _____   _____
12   loft   lock   _____   _____
13   quite   have   _____   _____
14   stool   fits   _____   _____

Give the missing letters and numbers in the following sequences. The alphabet has been written out to help you.

A B C D E F G H I J K L M N O P Q R S T U V W X Y Z

Example   CQ   DP   EQ   FP   GQ   <u>HP</u>

15	CF	CG	DH	DI	____	EK
16	____	vE	wF	xG	yH	zI
17	DW	EV	FU	____	HS	IR
18	AB	____	CF	DH	EJ	FL
19	OP	RQ	ST	VU	WX	____
20	W13	Y11	____	Y7	W5	Y3

17

Time for a break! Go to Puzzle Page 43

Total

Test 17: Mixed

Test time: 0 – 5 – 10 minutes

Fill in the crosswords so that all the given words are included.
You have been given one letter as a clue in each crossword.

1–3 SHARD STIFF FIXED SNOWS INDIA

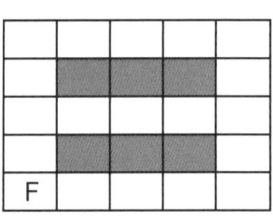

4–6 DARES ANGER BRAIN BEARD NOTES

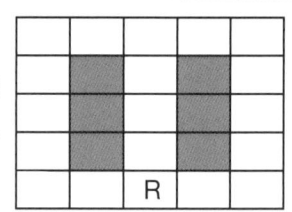

Underline the two words which are the odd ones out in the following groups of words.

Example   black   <u>king</u>   purple   green   <u>house</u>

7   hockey   cricket   ball   players   rounders
8   mouse   gerbil   rat   shark   cobra
9   oak   rose   sunflower   willow   tulip
10   book   television   newspaper   radio   magazine

Find the letter which will complete both pairs of words, ending the first word and starting the second. The same letter must be used for both pairs of words.

Example   mea (t) able   fi (t) ub

11   pin (__) ing   tal (__) ey
12   sta (__) elp   sill (__) es
13   pal (__) xam   to (__) agle
14   gri (__) ie   gras (__) ig

Here are some symbol codes for four words. Match the right code to the right word.

FADE   FIND   DEAN   NEED
! / @ %   @ £ £ %   ! * % £   % £ * @

15   FADE _____   16   FIND _____
17   DEAN _____   18   NEED _____

Using the same code, decode:

19   % / @ £ _____   20   % £ * ! _____

TEST 18: Mixed

Underline the one word in the brackets which will go equally well with both the pairs of words outside the brackets.

Example   rush, attack   cost, fee   (price, hasten, strike, <u>charge</u>, money)

1. fete, festival   even, just   (party, level, proper, fair, equal)
2. foolhardy, reckless   spots, redness   (rush, rash, acne, fever, silly)
3. build, construct   force, cause   (order, make, stack, assemble, form)
4. difficult, tough   firm, inflexible   (easy, solid, hard, complicated, strong)
5. copy, mimic   shadow, trail   (follow, model, stalk, obey, lead)

The drama club is putting on a school play. Tessa and Harriet are going to make the costumes. Nadeen and Ben are going to build the sets. Francesca is going to help with the costumes but also do the lights. Mick is going to be the announcer for the first half of the play and Tessa will be the announcer for the second half. Mick will also be in charge of moving the props on and off the stage. Ben will help Mick when he is busy as the announcer.

6. Which two students are doing only one job?   _____ and _____
7. Which student is helping with the costumes and the lights?   _____
8. How many students are helping make the costumes?   _____
9. Who will help move the props during the first half of the play?   _____
10. Which two students won't be busy during the play?   _____ and _____

Find the letter which will end the first word and start the second word.

Example   peac (h) ome

11. foo (__) humb   12. nex (__) rain   13. sta (__) elt   14. fee (__) ost

Rearrange the muddled letters in capitals to make a proper word. The answer will complete the sentence sensibly.

Example   A BEZAR is an animal with stripes.   ___ZEBRA___

15. Under the stairs there is a dark BOADRPUC.   _____
16. The moon was shining so BRGTYIHL, it lit up the room.   _____
17. Vijay's father parked the car in the GGREAA.   _____
18. Sixteen, seventeen, IHENEEGT, nineteen.   _____
19. A young goose is called a LNGGISO.   _____
20. My mother enjoys doing crossword ZSZLEPU.   _____

TEST 19: Mixed

Test time: 0 — 5 — 10 minutes

Underline the two words in each line which are most similar in type or meaning.

Example <u>dear</u> pleasant poor extravagant <u>expensive</u>

1 steer drive garden pond swift
2 wed flower marry church feast
3 son neighbour daughter friend student
4 hair heart arm neck leg
5 school scheme letter film plan

Change the first word into the last word, by changing one letter at a time and making a new, different word in the middle.

Example CASE <u>CASH</u> LASH

6 CUBE _____ TUNE
7 PALM _____ CALF
8 PINE _____ PICK
9 WARM _____ YARN

Fill in the missing letters and numbers. The alphabet has been written out to help you.

A B C D E F G H I J K L M N O P Q R S T U V W X Y Z

Example AB is to CD as PQ is to <u>RS</u>.

10 JK is to LM as NO is to ____.
11 S16 is to T14 as U12 is to ____.
12 FG3 is to GH5 as 7HI is to ____.
13 De is to Fg as Vw is to ____.
14 TR is to SQ as RP is to ____.
15 AD is to EH as IL is to ____.

Look at the first group of three words. The word in the middle has been made from the other two words. Complete the second group of three words in the same way, making a new word in the middle.

Example PA<u>IN</u> <u>INTO</u> <u>TO</u>OK   ALSO <u>SOON</u> ONLY

16 PEEL LOVE OVEN   BOSS _____ HUTS
17 INTO TORE REAP   MOTH _____ INCH
18 SHUN HUNT WILT   SPAT _____ FISH
19 STAR SOLD HOLD   MOOR _____ LICE
20 KIND KING RUNG   ZERO _____ NEST

20

Total

Test 20: Mixed

Underline the two words which are the odd ones out in the following groups of words.

Example black <u>king</u> purple green <u>house</u>

1. knife fork bowl plate spoon
2. stable cow elephant sheep sty
3. desk ruler class rubber pencil
4. spring rain winter snow summer
5. Australia Wales London Sweden Paris

Look at the first group of three words. The word in the middle has been made from the other two words. Complete the second group of three words in the same way, making a new word in the middle.

Example PA<u>IN</u> INTO TOOK ALSO __SOON__ ONLY

6. PAST STUN UNTO WIFE _____ ARCH
7. RAKE RUST MUST STAR _____ BEAT
8. DRAG DRIP SNIP FALL _____ SUNG
9. SPAR PART WENT TREE _____ HOOF
10. SLUG GONE ONES SLIM _____ AREA

Add one letter to the word in capital letters to make a new word. The meaning of the new word is given in the clue.

Example PLAN simple __plain__

11. RIGHT shiny _____
12. BUSH broom _____
13. TONE rock _____
14. FAME fire _____

15–20 Here are two rows of houses in a street. Work out which families live in each house.

22	24	26
ARMADA AVENUE		
21	23	25

The Bennetts and the Ashtons live directly next door to each other on the even side of the street.
The Bennetts live in a lower number than the Ashtons.
The Fish family live directly opposite the Catt family.
The Bennetts live directly opposite to the Smiths who live in a higher number than the Catts, next door.
The Jones family are best friends with the Fish family.

Bennett _____ Ashton _____ Fish _____

Catt _____ Smith _____ Jones _____

TEST 21: Mixed

Give the missing numbers and letters in the following sequences.

Example   2   4   6   8   10   _12_

1   14   24   ___   44   54   64
2   3   ___   11   15   19   23
3   ___   10   15   20   25   30
4   4   5   7   10   ___   19
5   X13   Y11   Z9   ___   Y5   Z3
6   64   32   16   8   4   ___

Solve the problems by working out the codes.

7   If x o – + is the code for DOWN, what does the code + o x stand for? _____
8   If < > / \ is the code for SANG, what does the code \ > < stand for? _____
9   If APPQ is DOOR, what does the code QPA stand for? _____
10   If = – ~ \ is the code for THIS, what does the code \ ~ = stand for? _____

Rearrange the letters in capitals to make another word. The new word has something to do with the first two words.

Example   spot   soil   SAINT   _STAIN_

11   loved   adored   READ   _____
12   light   fire   PARKS   _____
13   painful   hurting   ROSE   _____
14   killed   dead   NAILS   _____
15   frozen   water   DICE   _____
16   ruler   guide   DEALER   _____

Find a word that can be put in front of each of the following words to make new compound words.

Example   cast   fall   ward   pour   _down_

17   side   vent   to   sure   _____
18   knob   mat   step   bell   _____
19   times   where   thing   one   _____
20   world   wear   water   stand   _____

22

Test 22: Mixed

Find the three-letter word which can be added to the letters in capitals to make a new word. The new word will complete the sentence sensibly.

Example The cat sprang onto the MO. ___USE___

1. I hope we win some G medals at the Olympics. _____
2. My grandmother wears a HING aid. _____
3. Have a bowl of STBERRIES and cream. _____
4. Would you like jam and TER on your bread? _____
5. During the lunch H Tom plays football. _____

Underline the one word which **can be made** from the letters of the word in capital letters.

Example CHAMPION   camping   notch   peach   cramp   <u>chimp</u>

6	KINDEST	stink	desks	token	taste	kings
7	ELEPHANT	thank	neater	paler	panel	heaps
8	PARTITION	nation	print	parting	north	trains
9	CONTAINER	energy	conker	narrow	counter	ration
10	BRIGHTLY	height	truly	light	tight	highly

Remove one letter from the word in capital letters to leave a new word. The meaning of the new word is given in the clue.

Example AUNT   an insect   ___ANT___

11. DRIVE   plunge   _____
12. GRIND   smile   _____
13. BLAST   final   _____
14. TRANCE   copy   _____

Give the missing letters and numbers in the following sequences.
The alphabet has been written out to help you.

A B C D E F G H I J K L M N O P Q R S T U V W X Y Z

Example CQ   DP   EQ   FP   GQ   <u>HP</u>

15	Z12	Y10	X8	W6	V4	___
16	___	GW	HV	IU	JT	KS
17	MZ	MY	___	NW	OV	OU
18	kV	lU	mT	___	oR	pQ
19	Ny	___	Pw	Qv	Ru	St
20	AB	DC	EF	HG	___	LK

23

Total

TEST 23: Mixed

Test time: 0 — 5 — 10 minutes

Underline two words, one from each group, that go together to form a new word. The word in the first group always comes first.

Example (hand, <u>green</u>, for) (light, <u>house</u>, sure)

1. (hand, foot, close) (sore, writing, reading)
2. (dripping, wet, towel) (suit, clothes, tea)
3. (price, much, too) (more, kind, less)
4. (car, engine, wheel) (boot, near, barrow)

Give the missing numbers and letters in the following sequences.

Example 5 21 8 17 11 13 <u>14</u> 9

5	3	10	5	11	7	12	___	13	
6	___	r	9	s	12	t	15	u	
7	R15	R1	___	S2	T17	T3	U18	U4	
8	A7	1a	B7	2b	C7	3c	D7	___	
9	1	2	3	5	5	___	7	11	

Underline the pair of words most similar in meaning.

Example   come, go   <u>roam, wander</u>   ear, fare

10. whisper, shout   discuss, talk   argue, agree
11. block, lump   chunk, morsel   part, whole
12. up, down   outside, exterior   under, on
13. high, low   loud, faint   quiet, hushed
14. find, keep   enter, exit   fall, tumble

Change the first word of the third pair in the same way as the other pairs to give a new word.

Example   bind, hind   bare, hare   but, <u>hut</u>

15. wane, wean   pale, peal   bare, _____
16. top, lop   tight, light   tax, _____
17. pals, slap   deer, reed   draw, _____
18. made, dame   file, life   lope, _____
19. mean, mane   weak, wake   team, _____
20. chin, thin   chat, that   chose, _____

Test 1: Similars and Opposites (page 2)

1 **rigid, stiff** 'Rigid' and 'stiff' both mean hard, unbending.
2 **basin, bath** 'Basin' and 'bath' are both containers for water.
3 **apple, pear** 'Apple' and 'pear' are both fruit.
4 **clear, obvious** 'Clear' and 'obvious' both mean apparent.
5 **boat, yacht** 'Boat' and 'yacht' are forms of water transport whereas the others go on land.
6 **tidy, messy** 'Tidy' means neat so 'messy', which means untidy, is the most opposite in meaning.
7 **soft, hard** 'Soft' means gentle to touch so 'hard', which means tough or rigid, is the most opposite in meaning.
8 **solid, liquid** 'Solid' means hard with a definite form so 'liquid', which means runny with no definite form, is the most opposite in meaning.
9 **confident, shy** 'Confident' means self-assured so 'shy', which means unsure or nervous, is the most opposite in meaning.
10 **over, under** 'Over' means above so 'under', which means below, is the most opposite in meaning.
11 **complete, whole**
12 **grip, clasp**
13 **problem, difficulty**
14 **appear, arrive**
15 **feel, touch**
16 **take** To 'give' is to hand something over to someone whereas 'take' is to remove something from someone.
17 **bumpy** 'Flat' is smooth or level whereas 'bumpy' is uneven and up and down.
18 **above** 'Below' is under something whereas 'above' is over the top of something.
19 **dull** 'Shiny' means glossy or with a sheen whereas 'dull' is flat and non-reflective.
20 **beginning** 'End' is the finish or completion of something whereas the 'beginning' is at the start or onset.

Test 2: Sorting Words 1 (page 3)

1 **part** To 'part' is to leave behind something or someone and a 'part' is a section or slice of something.
2 **hit** To 'hit' is to strike and a 'hit' is something that is successful.
3 **trunk** A 'trunk' is a type of box or container and it can also mean the body or main part of something.
4 **bright** 'Bright' can mean shining and it can mean smart and quick to understand.
5 **plant** To 'plant' means to place or grow something in the ground and a 'plant' is a living thing with leaves.
6 **socks, shoes** These items are worn on the feet whereas the others are worn on the torso.
7 **bicycle, skateboard** These items are forms of land transport whereas the others are used on water.
8 **hat, glove** These items are clothing whereas the others are parts of the face.
9 **middle, bottom** These terms refer to a central part of something whereas the others are all on the edge or outside.
10 **sausage, sick** These terms are the odd ones out as all the others refer to safety and security.
11 **CONTINENTS**
12 **ELECTRIC**
13 **FRONT**
14 **SEASIDE**
15 **CHOCOLATE**
16 <u>Cows</u> give us <u>dairy</u> products.
17 Number <u>twenty</u> is on the <u>other</u> side of the street.
18 <u>You</u> were given <u>some</u> homework.
19 Can you close <u>the door</u> please?
20 My <u>shirt</u> is blue and <u>red</u>.

Test 3: Sorting Words 2 (page 4)

1 CHAIR
2 SPEND
3 PROOF
4 SHALLOW
5 WHEEL
6 shoe
7 lord
8 tell
9 stale
10 break
11 LANCE, CLEAN
12 SLOPE, POLES
13 FLAIR, FRAIL
14 WINGS, SWING
15 LEAST, TALES
16 SEAT
17 LEAP
18 ROPE
19 DROP
20 TEACH

Test 4: Selecting Words (page 5)

1 footpath
2 woodland
3 strawberry
4 handyman
5 whitewash
6 **y** play, yard
7 **k** think, king
8 **e** blue, eyes
9 **r** four, real
10 **w** flow, wind

11–15 Try each of the words in the first set of brackets. Do they make sense with any words in the second and third brackets? Only one combination of three words make sense.

11 **oars, rowed, shore**
12 **rocket, sky, station**
13 **drove, into, turned**
14 **uncle, mother's, brother**
15 **down, fragrant, garden**
16 **month** There is no 'h' in 'brainstorm'.
17 **bluff** There is only one 'f' in 'favourable'.
18 **argue** There is no 'u' in 'margarine'.
19 **quince** There is no 'c' in 'hindquarters'.
20 **brisk** There is no 'k' in 'crispbread'.

Test 5: Finding Words (page 6)

1 **form** Please wait <u>for me</u>.
2 **hiss** Your football team is good <u>this s</u>eason.
3 **hand** Jane painted her room peac<u>h and</u> cream.
4 **tore** I need <u>to re</u>member to lock the front door.
5 **belt** Please pin your la<u>bel t</u>o your jacket.
6 **AIR** hair
7 **DAY** holiday
8 **HUT** shut
9 **SHE** rushed
10 **OWL** bowl
11 **black** blackberry, blackboard, blackcurrant, blackbird
12 **hand** handcuff, handbag, handrail, handshake
13 **tea** teapot, teaspoon, teacake, teatime
14 **up** upstairs, upstream, upstanding, uproar
15 **life** lifeboat, lifebuoy, lifespan, lifeless
16 **a** fir, away
17 **m** arch, comb
18 **y** ever, yearly
19 **t** each, fleet
20 **c** limb, patch

Test 6: Alphabetical Order and Substitution (page 7)

1 **floor**
2 **hilly**
3 **adept**
4 **begins**
5 **deity**
6 **little** Look at the ends of the words. All of them end 'le'. Look at the previous letter and find the one that comes latest in the alphabet. Here, it is 't', so 'little' is the answer.
7 **galaxy** Look at the last letter of the words. Pick the one furthest from the start of the alphabet. Here, it is 'y', so 'galaxy' is the answer.
8 **fairness** Look at the ends of the words. All of them end in 'ness'. Look at the previous letter and find the one that comes latest in the alphabet. Here it is 'r', so 'fairness' is the answer.
9 **chariot** Look at the last letter of the words. All of them end in 't'. Look at the previous letter and find the one furthest from the start of the alphabet. Here it is 'o', so 'chariot' is the answer.
10 **tears** Look at the ends of the words. All of them end in 'ears'. Look at the first letter and find the one that comes latest in the alphabet. Here it is 't', so 'tears' is the answer.
11 **12** 13 − 1 = 12
12 **60** 10 × 6 = 60
13 **8** (10 − 8) + 6 = 8
14 **15** 8 + 6 + 1 = 15
15 **11** (13 − 8) + 6 = 11
16 **C** 10 − 5 = 5. C = 5
17 **E** 3 + 2 + 5 = 10. E = 10.
18 **B** 6 ÷ 2 = 3. B = 3.
19 **A** 10 − (3 + 5) = 2. A = 2.
20 **D** 2 × 3 = 6. D = 6.

Test 7: Word Progressions (page 8)

1–5 Use grids as shown below to help work out the missing word.

1 **TREE**

		1	2	3	4			1				2	3	4
F	E	E	S		I	N	K	Y		P	O	S	T		R	E	E	K

2 **STAR**

		1	2		3	4				1	2		3	4
D	E	A	R		C	H	I	P		M	O	S	T		A	R	M	Y

3 **EAST**

1	2	3					4		1	2	3					4
B	O	A	T		P	I	N	S		P	E	A	S		G	O	A	T

4 **CLAM**

1					2	3	4		1						2	3	4
G	E	A	R		W	O	L	F		C	R	O	W		S	L	A	M

5 **EXIT**

1	2				3	4		1	2					3	4
P	A	R	T		W	I	N	E		E	X	A	M		K	N	I	T

6 **BIND**
7 **TALK**
8 **BELL**
9 **SING**
10 **FARE**
11 **seal** In each pair, the fourth letter of the first word is placed as the second letter of the last word, so 'sale' becomes 'seal'.
12 **felt** In each pair, the first and third letters of the first word are swapped in the last word, so 'left' becomes 'felt'.
13 **rail** In each pair, the 'f' becomes 'r', so 'fail' becomes 'rail'.
14 **fall** In each pair, the 'w' becomes 'f', so 'wall' becomes 'fall'.

15 **peek** In each pair, the letters are reversed, so 'keep' becomes 'peek'.
16–20 Solve these questions by looking at the first set of three and working out how the first and last numbers have been used to arrive at the middle number. Apply this to the second set of three and see if it works. If it does, apply it to the last set.
16 **16** 7 + 8 = 15 and 6 + 3 = 9, so 13 + 3 = 16
17 **2** 2 ÷ 2 = 1 and 4 ÷ 2 = 2, so 6 ÷ 3 = 2
18 **15** 4 x 2 = 8 and 4 x 3 = 12, so 3 x 5 = 15
19 **8** 13 − 11 = 2 and 21 − 12 = 9, so 16 − 8 = 8
20 **20** 3 x 3 = 9 and 8 x 2 = 16, so 5 x 4 = 20

Test 8: Logic (page 9)

1–2 **Tiles are a type of roof covering. A house needs a roof.** Use only the information you are given. Not all roofs are made of tiles nor do all houses have tiles. Straw is not mentioned.
3–4 **Helmets may be a part of a police officer's uniform. Police officers help to catch people who break the law.** Use only the information you are given. Not all the police wear helmets. Pairs are not mentioned nor whether people feel safe or not.

5–9

HUTCH 1	HUTCH 2	HUTCH 3	HUTCH 4	HUTCH 5
Floppy eared	Brown & white	White	Black	Fat

The floppy eared rabbit is either in Hutch 1 or 5. Later in the information, you learn that this rabbit is to the left of another, therefore the floppy eared rabbit is in Hutch 1. In the final sentence you learn the brown & white (2) is between the floppy eared (1) and white rabbit (3). The black rabbit is next to the white rabbit and that means the fat rabbit is in Hutch 5.

10–14 A table is the easiest way to sort the information, like this:

	Football	Cricket	Rugby	Computer Games
Sam	✓		✓	✓
Otis	✓			✓
Bob	✓	✓		✓
Mike	✓	✓	✓	✓
Ravi	✓			
Tom			✓	✓

10 **Mike**
11 **5**
12 **Tom**
13 **1**
14 **Sam**

15–20

A PHOTOGRAPHS	B DVDs
C CDs	D NOVELS
E SCHOOL BOOKS	F REFERENCE BOOKS

The novels are not on the bottom shelf (E or F) and if they are right of the CDs, they must be either B or D. Later, it mentions that the DVDs are above the novels. This means the novels are **D** and the DVDs are **B**. The CDs are **C** as the novels are directly to the right of the CDs and the reference books must be **F** as the novels are directly above them. This leaves the photographs and the school books. The CDs are higher than the school books, so they must be E and the photographs must be **A**.

Test 9: Codes (page 10)

1–5 All the words begin with B except KIND, so B = 6 and K = 0. So, KIND = 0138. BIND has three letters the same as KIND so BIND = 6138. Knowing these number and letter pairings will allow you to work out the rest.
1 **6538** B = 6, E = 5, N = 3, D = 8
2 **6138** B = 6, I = 1, N = 3, D = 8
3 **6440** B = 6, O = 4, K = 0
4 **0138** K = 0, I = 1, N = 3, D = 8
5 **DONE** 8 = D, 4 = O, 3 = N, 5 = E
6 **FOR** 7 = F, 9 = O, 4 = R
7 **CAME** 1 = C, 6 = A, 5 = M, 2 = E
8 **ROPE** 6 = R, 4 = O, 9 = P, 1 = E
9 **RAT** 1 = R, 8 = A, 3 = T
10 **MET** 7 = M, 2 = E, 6 = T
11 **CJUT** To get from the word to the code, move each letter forwards one place.
12 **OCUV** To get from the word to the code, move each letter forwards two places.
13 **CFFO** To get from the word to the code, move each letter forwards one place.
14 **GDDK** To get from the word to the code, move each letter backwards one place.
15 **DMSJ** To get from the word to the code, move each letter backwards two places.
16 **MADE** To get from the code to the word, move each letter backwards three places.
17 **NEED** To get from the code to the word, move each letter backwards four places.
18 **GERM** To get from the code to the word, move each letter forwards one place.
19 **DEEP** To get from the code to the word, move each letter forwards two places.
20 **BITE** To get from the code to the word, move each letter forwards one place.

Test 10: Sequences (page 11)

1. **vein, blood** A 'river' carries 'water' in the same way as a 'vein' carries 'blood'.
2. **summer, hot** 'Winter' is 'cold' in the same way as 'summer' is 'hot'.
3. **gills, lungs** 'Fish' breathe with 'gills' in the same way as a 'man' breathes with 'lungs'.
4. **start, finish** 'Begin' is similar to 'start' in the same way as 'end' is to 'finish'.
5. **break, stop** 'Pause' is similar to 'break' in the same way as 'halt' is to 'stop'.
6. **WU** Each letter in the first pair moves backwards by one letter in the second pair.
7. **Pt** Each letter in the first pair moves forwards by five letters in the second pair.
8. **YZ** Each letter in the first pair moves forward by two letters in the second pair.
9. **M9** The letter in the first pair moves backwards by one letter in the second pair. The number in the first pair increases by 2 in the second pair.
10. **NP** Each letter in the first pair moves forward by two letters in the second pair.
11. **4** The number decreases by 4 each time.
12. **12** The number added increases by 1 each time: +1, +2, +3, +4, +5
13. **9** The number increases by 4 each time.
14. **303** The number increases by 101 each time.
15. **23v** The number increases by 2 each time. The letter is in a repeating pattern: ttuuvv.
16. **IM** The first letter in each pair moves forward by two letter in the next pair. The second letter moves forward by one letter in the next pair.
17. **NP** The first letter in each pair moves forward by one letter in the next pair. The second letter moves forward by two letters in the next pair.
18. **QS** The first letter is in a repeating pattern: PPQQRR. The second letter in each pair moves forward by one letter in the next pair.
19. **QP** The first letter is in a repeating pattern: PQPQPQ. The second letter moves backwards by two letters in the next pair.
20. **Ht** The first letter in each pair moves forward by one letter in the next pair. The second letter moves backwards by one letter in the next pair.

Test 11: Mixed (page 12)

1. **RUBBER**
2. **BUCKET**
3. **JANUARY**
4. **STING**
5. **EXPLOSION**
6. **CHRISTMAS**
7. **ACEILPS** Write the word 'SPECIAL' down. Starting with the 'A', write each letter in alphabetical order, crossing it off in 'SPECIAL' as you go.
8. **L**
9. **ACEHPR** Write the word 'PREACH' down. Starting with the 'A', write each letter in alphabetical order, crossing it off in 'PREACH' as you go.
10. **H**
11. **stain**
12. **fear**
13. **store**
14. **save**
15. **vile**
16. **NPQR** S = N, E = P, A = Q, M = R
17. **FERNN** S = F, T = E, A = R, L = N
18. **342** T = 3, I = 4, E = 2
19. **zvb** S = z, I = v, T = b
20. **YTRX** P = Y, L = T, U = R, M = X

Test 12: Mixed (page 13)

1–4 Arrange the words in a grid to make it easier to put them in reverse alphabetical order.

1. **brooch**

b	r	o	o	c	h		2nd
b	r	e	a	k			4th
b	r	a	c	k	e	n	5th
b	r	u	i	s	e		1st
b	r	i	d	g	e		3rd

2. **chimney**

c	h	i	m	n	e	y	2nd
c	h	o	o	s	e		1st
c	h	e	r	u	b		3rd
c	h	e	e	k			4th
c	h	a	p	e	l		5th

3. **penny**

p	e	n	g	u	i	n	3rd
p	e	d	a	l			4th
p	e	n	n	y			2nd
p	e	o	n	y			1st
p	e	c	a	n			5th

4. **danger**

d	a	r	k	n	e	s	s	1st
d	a	n	g	e	r			2nd
d	a	n	c	i	n	g		3rd
d	a	m	p	e	n			4th
d	a	i	n	t	y			5th

5. **SEAT** 1 = S, 6 = E, 4 = A, 8 = T
6. **DOG** 6 = D, 9 = O, 3 = G

7 **TIME** 5 = T, 7 = 1, 6 = M, 2 = E
8 **BAR** 1 = B, 9 = A, 4 = R
9 **horse** A 'kennel' is a home to a 'dog' in the same way as a 'stable' is to a 'horse'.
10 **bed** A 'cushion' goes on a 'chair' in the same way as a 'pillow' goes on a 'bed'.
11 **two** A 'butterfly' has six legs in the same way as a 'bird' has 'two' legs.
12 **floor** A 'picture' is hung on the 'wall' in the same way a 'rug' goes on the 'floor'.
13–16 Draw a square, if necessary, to help you and the compass points.

Town D   Town A

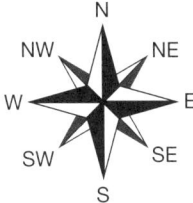

Town C   Town B

From the information, you know B is south of A but east of C. D is north of C.
13 **west**
14 **north-east**
15 **north-west**
16 **south-east**
17 **E** 24 ÷ 12 = 2, E = 2
18 **A** 12 + 8 + 4 = 24, A = 24
19 **C** (12 − 8) + 4 = 8, C = 8
20 **D** (4 × 2) ÷ 2 = 4, D = 4

Test 13: Mixed (page 14)

1 **ROW** crown   2 **FOR** forks
3 **HOP** shop   4 **HER** where
5 **OWE** power   6 **p** pass, pink, pray, pat
7 **s** show, sat, seven, sand
8 **f** four, foal, fox, fear
9 **o** open, orange, oat, omen
10 **ST** Each letter in the first pair moves forward by four letters in the second pair.
11 **PR** Each letter in the first pair moves forward by four letters in the second pair.
12 **J11** The letter moves backwards by one letter and the number increases by 1.
13 **Yz** Each letter in the first pair moves forward by four letters in the second pair.
14 **NL** Each letter in the first pair moves backwards by four letters in the second pair.
15 **MN** Each letter in the first pair moves backwards by two letters in the second pair.
16 **path** 'Trail' and 'path' both mean a track or a route.
17 **praise** 'Honour' and 'praise' both mean admire and acclaim.
18 **fuel** 'Petrol' is a type of 'fuel'.
19 **find** 'Discover' and 'find' both mean to come across something you may be searching for.
20 **red** 'Crimson' is a type of 'red' colour.

Test 14: Mixed (page 15)

1 **conceal, mask** Both words mean to hide or disguise something.
2 **menace, threaten** Both words mean to endanger or intend harm.
3 **skin, peel** Both words are the covering of a person or fruit, for example.
4 **tune, melody** Both words mean the music part of a song.
5 **miserable, sad** Both words mean unhappy.
6–11 Two of the words begin with B, so B = X. The double OO in BOOT means that the code must be X 5 5 ?. From these, you can work out the rest.
6 **X 5 5 ?** B = X, O = 5, T = ?
7 **X Q 5 £** B = X, R = Q, O = 5, W = £
8 **? Q + =** T = ?, R = Q, A = +, Y = =
9 **£ + Q =** W = £, A = +, R = Q, Y = =
10 **WART** £ = W, + = A, Q = R, ? = T
11 **ROOT** Q = R, O = 5, ? = T
12 **3** This is an alternating pattern. The first, third, fifth and seventh increase by 2 each time. The second, fourth, sixth and eighth increase by 3 each time.
13 **Q14** The letter is in a repeating pattern: QBQBQBQB. The number is in an alternating pattern. The first, third, fifth and seventh increase by 2 each time. The second, fourth, sixth and eighth increase by 1 each time.
14 **b15** The letter is in a repeating pattern: aabbccdd. The number is in an alternating pattern. The first, third, fifth and seventh decrease by 2 each time. The second, fourth, sixth and eighth increase by 1 each time.
15 **28** The number decreases by 7 each time. The letter moves forward by two places each time.
16 **7** This is an alternating pattern. The first, third, fifth and seventh increases by 3 each time. The second, fourth, sixth and eighth increases by 2 each time.
17 **10** (14 ÷ 2) + 3 = 10
18 **2** 14 − (3 × 4) = 2
19 **9** (15 ÷ 3) + 4 = 9
20 **20** 14 + (2 × 3) = 20

Test 15: Mixed (page 16)

1. F<u>R</u>EED
2. FI<u>R</u>ST
3. LE<u>A</u>NT
4. <u>L</u>EAVES
5. **ZBSE** To get from the word to the code, move each letter forwards one place.
6. **YKPF** To get from the word to the code, move each letter forwards two places.
7. **QMAI** To get from the word to the code, move each letter backwards two places.
8. **ADRS** To get from the word to the code, move each letter backwards one place.
9. **QFMC** To get from the word to the code, move each letter backwards two places.
10. **HCKN** To get from the word to the code, move each letter forwards two places.
11. **life** In each pair, the first three letters of the first word is reversed, so 'file' becomes 'life'.
12. **book** In each pair, the first letter changes from 'r' to 'b', so 'rook' becomes 'book'.
13. **leak** In each pair, the first letter remains the same. The fourth letter becomes the second followed by the other two, so 'lake' becomes 'leak'.
14. **drip** In each pair, the first letter changes from 't' to 'd', so 'trip' becomes 'drip'.
15. **went** In each pair, the first and the third letters change place, so 'newt' becomes 'went'.
16. **wolf** In each pair, the letters reverse, so 'flow' becomes 'wolf'.
17. **7** $15 - 8 = 7$
18. **19** $(12 + 8) - 1 = 19$
19. **5** $15 \div 3 = 5$
20. **7** $(12 - 8) + 3 = 7$

Test 16: Mixed (page 17)

1. **engine** There is only one 'n' in 'gaberdine'.
2. **saddle** There is no 'e' in 'dastardly'.
3. **police** There is no 'c' in 'apologise'.
4. **wasps** There is only one 's' in 'newspaper'.
5. **arrest** There is no 'e' or double 's' in 'apparatus'.
6. **them** Mum buys fruit at <u>the m</u>arket.
7. **star** That is my be<u>st ar</u>rangement today.
8. **than** I will brush my tee<u>th an</u>other time.
9. **swan** Half the clas<u>s wan</u>dered in late.
10. **shun** Must I br<u>ush un</u>der the desks too?
11. **l** pay, slap
12. **f** lot, flock
13. **e** quit, heave
14. **s** tool, fists
15. **EJ** The first letter is in a repeating pattern: CCDDEE. The second letter moves forward by one letter in the next pair.
16. **uD** Each letter moves forwards by one letter in the next pair.
17. **GT** The first letter moves forward by one letter in the next pair. The second letter moves backwards by one letter in the next pair.
18. **BD** The first letter moves forward by one letter in the next pair. The second letter moves forwards by two letters.
19. **ZY** This is a repeating pattern. The letters are in alphabetical order but the second, fourth, sixth and eighth pairs are reversed.
20. **W9** The letters are in a repeating pattern: WYWYWY. The numbers decrease by 2 each time.

Test 17: Mixed (page 18)

1–3    4–6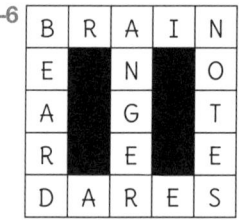

7. **ball, players** The other three are games.
8. **shark, cobra** The other three are mammals or rodents.
9. **oak, willow** The other three are flowers.
10. **television, radio** The other three communicate using written words.
11. **k** pink, king; talk, key
12. **y** stay, yelp; silly, yes
13. **e** pale, exam; toe, eagle
14. **p** grip, pie; grasp, pig
15–20 'NEED' has double 'e'. Therefore, its code is @ £ £ %. Two of the words begin with 'F'. You know D = %, so FADE = ! * % £. You can now work out the other codes.
15. **! * % £** F = !, A = *, D = %, E = £
16. **! / @ %** F = !, I = /, N = @, D = %
17. **% £ * @** D = %, E = £, A = *, N = @
18. **@ £ £ %** N = @, E = £, D = %
19. **DINE** % = D, / = I, @ = N, £ = E
20. **DEAF** % = D, £ = E, * = A, ! = F

Test 18: Mixed (page 19)

1. **fair** A 'fair' is a celebration and also means to be impartial and unbiased.
2. **rash** To be 'rash' is impetuous or hasty; a rash is also a form of skin irritation.
3. **make** To 'make' is to compose or create; it also means to form or cause to happen.
4. **hard** If something is 'hard' it can be tricky to do; it also means rigid or unbending.

5 **follow** 'Follow' means to imitate as well as to track or stalk.
6–10 A table is the easiest way to sort the information, like this:

	Make costumes	Build sets	Lights	Announcer	Move props
Tessa				✓ (2nd half)	
Harriet	✓				
Nadeen		✓			
Ben		✓		✓ (1st half)	
Francesca	✓		✓		
Mick				✓ (1st half)	✓

6 **Harriet and Nadeen**
7 **Francesca**
8 **3**
9 **Ben**
10 **Harriet and Nadeen**
11 **t** foot, thumb
12 **t** next, train
13 **b** stab, belt
14 **l** feel, lost
15 **CUPBOARD**
16 **BRIGHTLY**
17 **GARAGE**
18 **EIGHTEEN**
19 **GOSLING**
20 **PUZZLES**

Test 19: Mixed (page 20)

1 **steer, drive** Both words mean to guide or direct.
2 **wed, marry** Both words mean a couple making a long term commitment to another.
3 **son, daughter** Both words mean a sibling.
4 **arm, leg** Both are words for limbs.
5 **scheme, plan** Both these words mean an idea, or method or proposal.
6 **TUBE**
7 **CALM**
8 **PINK**
9 **WARN**
10 **PQ** Each letter in the first pair moves forward by two letters in the second pair.
11 **V10** The letter in the first pair moves forward one letter in the second pair and the number decreases by 2.
12 **IJ9** The letters in the first pair are consecutive with the second letter repeated, so 'HI' becomes 'IJ'. The number increases by 2.
13 **Xy** Each letter in the first pair moves forward by two letters in the second pair.
14 **QO** Each letter in the first pair moves backwards one place in the second pair.
15 **MP** Each letter in the first pair moves forward by four letters in the second pair.
16–20 Use grids as shown below to help work out the missing word.
16 **SHUT**

	1	2	3	4		1	2	3	4
P	E	E	L		O	V	E	N

	1	2	3	4
B	O	S	S

	2	3	4
H	U	T	S

17 **THIN**

	1	2	3	4		1	2	3	4
I	N	T	O	R	E	A	P

	1	2	3	4		3	4
M	O	T	H	I	N	C	H

18 **PATH**

	1	2	3		4
S	H	U	N	W	I	L	T

	1	2	3		4
S	P	A	T	F	I	S	H

19 **MICE**

1					2	3	4
S	T	A	R	H	O	L	D

1					2	3	4
M	O	O	R	L	I	C	E

20 **ZEST**

1	2				3	4
K	I	N	D	R	U	N	G

1	2				3	4
Z	E	R	O	N	E	S	T

Test 20: Mixed (page 21)

1 **bowl, plate** The other words are utensils you eat with.
2 **stable, sty** The other words are animals.
3 **desk, class** The other words are items of stationery.
4 **rain, snow** The other words are seasons.
5 **London, Paris** The other words are countries.
6–10 Use grids as shown below to help work out the missing word.
6 **FEAR**

	1	2	3	4		1	2	3	4
P	A	S	T	U	N	T	O

	1	2	3	4
W	I	F	E

	1	2	3	4
A	R	C	H

7 **SEAT**

1					2	3	4
R	A	K	E	M	U	S	T

1					2	3	4
S	T	A	R	B	E	A	T

8 **FANG**

1	2				3	4
D	R	A	G	S	N	I	P

1	2				3	4
F	A	L	L	S	U	N	G

9 **REEF**

1	2	3				4
S	P	A	R	W	E	N	T

1	2	3				4
T	R	E	E	H	O	O	F

10 **MARE**

	1				2	3	4
S	L	U	G	O	N	E	S

	1				2	3	4
S	L	I	M	A	R	E	A

11 **BRIGHT**
12 **BRUSH**
13 **STONE**
14 **FLAME**

15–20

22 Fish	24 Bennett	26 Ashton

ARMADA AVENUE

21 Catt	23 Smith	25 Jones

The Bennetts live in either 22 or 24 as they live in an even numbered house, next door to the Ashtons, who live in a higher numbered house (24 or 26). The Fish family live opposite the Catt family and you know the Catts are an odd numbered house, so the Fish family must live in 22 or 26 and the Catts in 21 or 25. If the Bennetts are opposite the Smiths and the Smiths are in a higher numbered house than the Catts, then the Catts must be in 21, the Fish family in 22, the Bennetts in 24 and the Ashtons in 26. The Smiths are opposite the Bennetts, so are in 23, leaving the Jones family in 25.

Test 21: Mixed (page 22)

1. **34** The numbers increase by 10.
2. **7** The numbers increase by 4.
3. **5** The numbers increase by 5.
4. **14** The number added increases by 1 each time: +1, +2, +3, +4, +5
5. **X7** The letters are in a repeating pattern: XYZXYZ. The numbers decrease by 2.
6. **2** Each number is half the value of the preceding one.
7. **NOD** + = N, o = O, x = D
8. **GAS** \ = G, > = A, < = S
9. **ROD** Q = R, P = O, A = D
10. **SIT** \ = S, ~ = I, = = T
11. **DEAR**   12. **SPARK**
13. **SORE**   14. **SLAIN**
15. **ICED**   16. **LEADER**
17. **in** inside, invent, into, insure
18. **door** doorknob, doormat, doorstep, doorbell
19. **some** sometimes, somewhere, something, someone
20. **under** underworld, underwear, underwater, understand

Test 22: Mixed (page 23)

1. **OLD** gold   2. **EAR** hearing
3. **RAW** strawberries 4. **BUT** butter
5. **OUR** hour   6. stink
7. panel   8. print
9. ration   10. light
11. **DIVE**   12. **GRIN**
13. **LAST**   14. **TRACE**
15. **U2** The letter moves backwards one place. The numbers decrease by 2.
16. **FX** The first letter moves forward by one place. The second letter moves backwards one place.
17. **NX** The first letter is in a repeating pattern: MMNNOO. The second letter moves backwards one place.
18. **nS** The first letter moves forwards one place. The second letter moves backwards one place.
19. **Ox** The first letter moves forwards one place. The second letter moves backwards one place.
20. **IJ** The pairs of letters are in a repeating pattern. The letters are in alphabetical order but the second, fourth and sixth are reversed.

Test 23: Mixed (page 24)

1. **handwriting**   2. **wetsuit**
3. **priceless**   4. **wheelbarrow**
5. **9** This is an alternating pattern. The first, third, fifth and seventh numbers increase by 2. The second, fourth, sixth and eighth numbers increase by 1.
6. **6** This is an alternating pattern. The numbers increase by 3. The letters move forwards one place.
7. **S16** The letters are in a repeating pattern: RRSSTTUU. The numbers are in an alternating pattern. The first, third, fifth and seventh numbers increase by 1 (15, 16, 17, 18). The second, fourth, sixth and eighth numbers also increase by 1 (1, 2, 3, 4).
8. **4d** The letters are in a repeating pattern: AaBbCcDd. The numbers are in an alternating pattern. The first, third, fifth and seventh numbers are 7 each time. The second, fourth, sixth and eighth numbers increase by 1.
9. **8** This is an alternating pattern. The first, third, fifth and seventh numbers increase by 2. The second, fourth, sixth and eighth numbers increase by 3.
10. discuss, talk
11. block, lump
12. outside, exterior
13. quiet, hushed
14. fall, tumble
15. **bear** The final letter of the first word becomes the second letter in the second word.
16. **lax** The 't' at the beginning of the first word becomes 'l'.
17. **ward** The second word is the first word reversed.
18. **pole** The first three letters of the first word are reversed in the second word.
19. **tame** The second letter of the first word is placed at the end of the second word.
20. **those** The 'c' at the beginning of the first word is replaced with 't'.

Test 24: Mixed (page 25)

1. **8F9** Both the numbers in each trio increase by 1. The letters move forward by one place.
2. **13** The numbers increase by 4 each time.
3. **17** The numbers increase by 2 each time.
4. **15H** The numbers increase by 5 each time. The letters are in a repeating pattern: HHGGFF.
5. **love** The policeman's helmet fell **ove**r his eyes.
6. **item** She gave me my favour**ite m**agazine.
7. **sour** We will mi**s our** turn.
8. **thin** The twins are bo**th in** the show.
9. **them** "Best foot forwards!" shouted **the m**ajor.
10. **shoot**, **fire** Both words mean to let off a gun.
11. **train, teach** Both words mean to educate, to help to learn.
12. **pair, two** Both words mean more than one and less than three.
13. **diary, journal** Both words mean a book that you write dates or appointments in or record what has happened.
14. **road, street** Both words mean a highway or track that cars usually go on.
15. **MBOE** To get from the word to the code, move each letter forwards one place.
16. **LHMS** To get from the word to the code, move each letter backwards one place.
17. **PCKN** To get from the word to the code, move each letter forwards two places.
18. **CDRJ** To get from the word to the code, move each letter backwards one place.
19. **CBMM** To get from the word to the code, move each letter forwards one place.
20. **EPGB** To get from the word to the code, move each letter backwards two places.

Test 25: Mixed (page 26)

1. **kind, cruel** 'Kind' means caring and gentle whereas 'cruel' means unkind.
2. **more, less** 'More' means a little extra whereas 'less' means a little smaller or fewer.
3. **clean, dirty** 'Clean' means spotless whereas 'dirty' means unclean or messy.
4. **answer, question** 'Answer' means reply whereas 'question' means to ask.
5. **Turn** over your papers and **begin**.
6. There **were** over thirty children **at** the party.
7. The **television** will not change **channels**.
8. He watered the **garden** with a **hose**.
9. Edith **spread** butter on her **burnt** toast.
10. Sometimes I push my little **sister** on the **swing**.
11. **25** This is an alternating pattern. The first, third, fifth and seventh number increases by 1. The second, fourth, sixth and eighth number decreases by 5.
12. **15e** The numbers are in an alternating pattern. The first, third, fifth and seventh number increases by 2. The second, fourth, sixth and eighth number decreases by 5. The letters are in a repeating pattern: eyeyeyey.
13. **20** The letters and numbers alternate. The missing number is 20 because the numbers increase by 3.
14. **9** This is an alternating pattern. The first, third, fifth and seventh numbers decrease by 2. The second, fourth, sixth and eighth numbers decrease by 3.
15. **A3** The letters are in a repeating pattern: AXAXAXAX. The numbers are in an alternating pattern. The first, third, fifth and seventh numbers go down by 2. The second, fourth, sixth and eighth numbers remain as 5.
16. **PARTS, STRAP**
17. **LEAPT, PLATE**
18. **SPOOL, LOOPS**
19. **DEALER, LEADER**
20. **STEAL, LEAST**

Test 26: Mixed (page 27)

1–5 Use grids as shown below to help work out the missing word.

1 PLAY

	1	2	3	4			1	2	3	4
K	I	N	D		R	O	P	E		
D	E	E	P		L	A	Y	S		

2 EATS

1	2	3				4	1	2	3			4
D	R	A	G		F	I	N	E				
N	E	A	T		C	A	T	S				

3 FOOL

1			2	3	4	1			2	3	4
W	A	N	T		F	I	R	E			
F	O	O	T		T	O	O	L			

4 ONCE

	1	2		3	4		1	2	3	4
L	A	T	E		S	T	O	W		
M	O	O	N		C	E	N	T		

5 SNOW

1		2			3	4	1		2		3	4
P	I	N	E		W	H	A	T				
S	T	U	N		F	L	O	W				

6. **fast** The word most opposite to 'SLOW' is 'fast' as it means moving quickly.
7. **straightforward** The word most opposite to 'TRICKY' is 'straightforward' as it means uncomplicated.
8. **correct** The word most opposite to 'WRONG' is 'correct' as it means right.
9. **frequent** The word most opposite to 'RARE' is 'frequent' as it means happening often.

10 **mature** The word most opposite to 'IMMATURE' is 'mature' which means ripe, or grown up.
11 **t** teach, touch, tear, thigh
12 **h** hour, hill, hearth, hair
13 **s** smile, stuck, spill, spin
14 **l** lice, ledge, learn, late
15 **EG** Both letters of the first pair move forward one place.
16 **JI** Both letters of the first pair move backwards two places.
17 **Rs** Both letters move forward two places.
18 **NL** Both letters move backwards one place.
19 **9TU** The numbers decrease by 2. Both the letters move forwards by one letter.
20 **W55** The letter moves forward by one place. The number increases by 11.

Test 27: Mixed (page 28)

1 relaxed, strict
2 soft, firm
3 wealthy, poor
4 stale, fresh
5–10 Try each of the words in the first set of brackets. Do they make sense with any words in the second and third brackets? Only one combination of three words make sense.
5 elephants, river, trunks
6 road, right, traffic
7 ran, ball, goal
8 playground, put on, coats
9 pencil, over, bin
10 exciting, book, chapter
11 **5** 10 ÷ 2 = 5
12 **6** (1 x 2) + 4 = 6
13 **1** (3 x 1) – 2 = 1
14 **40** 10 x 4 = 40
15 **WEED** To get from the code to the word, move each letter forwards two places.
16 **FIRM** To get from the code to the word, move each letter forwards one place.
17 **HURT** To get from the code to the word, move each letter backwards two places.
18 **FOUR** To get from the code to the word, move each letter backwards one place.
19 **LIFE** To get from the code to the word, move each letter forwards one place.
20 **BIRD** To get from the code to the word, move each letter backwards one place.

Test 28: Mixed (page 29)

1 PEACH, CHEAP
2 TOAST, STOAT
3 TRACE, CRATE
4 ASLEEP, PLEASE
5 STATE, TASTE
6 **beef, cow** 'Venison' is deer meat as 'beef' is cow meat.
7 **radio, listen** You 'watch' 'television' in the way you 'listen' to the 'radio'.
8 **black, grey** 'Pink' is a whiter shade of 'red' as 'grey' is a whiter shade of 'black'.
9 **dawn, dusk** 'Sunrise' is at the beginning of a day as 'sunset' is at the end. 'Dawn' is at 'sunrise' as 'dusk' is at 'sunset'.
10 **apple, fruit** A 'carrot' is a 'vegetable' as an 'apple' is a 'fruit'.
11 **bedroom, sleep** A 'kitchen' is where you 'cook'. A 'bedroom' is where you 'sleep'.
12–15 A table is the easiest way to sort the information, like this.

	Spelling books	Library books	Photo album	Maths books	Reading books
Ann	✓	✓			✓
Mira	✓			✓	
Chloe	✓			✓	✓
Davina		✓			✓
Beth			✓		✓

12 Ann
13 Beth
14 Chloe
15 3
16 **LOMN** If the code for C = L, H = O, A = M and T = N, then CHAT = LOMN.
17 **TRA** If the code for S = T, O = R and B = A, then SOB = TRA.
18 **SBYF** If the code for R = S, O = B, T = Y and A = F, then ROTA = SBYF.
19 **AZC** If the code for A = A, R = Z, T = C, then ART = AZC.
20 **WZTL** If the code for P = W, A = Z, C = T and T = L, then PACT = WZTL.

Test 29: Mixed (page 30)

1 **b** crab, boxes
2 **l** girl, last
3 **s** dogs, soup
4 **h** bath, harp
5–8 Use the first letter as an indicator. If any of the later letters come earlier in the alphabet, you can reject that word straight away. Then look carefully through at the remaining words.
5 **first** The first three words all have letters earlier in the alphabet than 'f'. It is not 'fusion' as 'u' is the second letter and later in the alphabet than the following letters, therefore it is 'first'.
6 **accent** Two of the words have 'a' later in the word. Both 'alert' and 'agent' have an 'e' after a later letter, therefore it is 'accent'.

7 **blot** All the words start 'bl'. Two words have earlier letters than 'l' later in the word. 'Bloom' has 'm' after 'oo'. 'Blown' has 'n' after 'w'. Therefore, it is 'blot'.

8 **hilly** 'Hinge' and 'height' have 'e' after the 'h'. 'Humus' has 'u' near the beginning of a word. 'Hippo' has 'o' after 'p', therefore it is 'hilly'.

9–12 Quickly number one to ten and put the letters down to help you answer these questions.

1	2	3	4	5	6	7	8	9	10
A	B	C	D	E	F	G	H	I	J

9 **JADE** 10 = J, 1 = A, 4 = D, 5 = E
10 **ICED** 9 = I, 3 = C 5 = E, 4 = D
11 **6145** F = 6, A = 1, D = 4, E = 5
12 **8554** H = 8, E = 5, D = 4

13–14 **Cars travel on roads. Roads are for vehicles to travel on.** Rely only on the information you are given. The statements 'Only vans travel on the road' and 'All vehicles are cars' are not true as we are told 'Cars and vans are vehicles' and 'All vehicles travel on the road'. 'Vans drive fast' may or may not be true. This must be rejected as it is not mentioned.

15–16 **My cat is related to a lion. The cat family includes tigers.** Rely only on the information you are given. 'My cat is a lion' is not mentioned in the information so must be rejected. 'All cats are tigers' is not true as we are told lions are also members of the cat family. 'Lions eat tigers' may or may not be true. This must be rejected as it is not mentioned.

17 **6** The number added increases by 1 each time: +1, +2, +3, +4, +5
18 **11** The number increases by 4 each time.
19 **22** The number increases by 2 each time.
20 **12** The number decreases by 2 each time.

Test 30: Mixed (page 31)

1 **At** the bottom of the garden there **is** a shed.
2 The **bus** stopped at the bottom of the **road**.
3 Jake **had** eggs and bacon **for** breakfast.
4 **Please go** to bed now.
5 The **leaves** fell off the **trees**.
6 She **put** her fork and knife **in** the dishwasher.
7 **wholesome**
8 **upset**
9 **indeed**
10 **windscreen**
11–15 Two words begin with 'M', so 'M' must be 1. 1446 is therefore MEET because of the double letter/ number. From this information, you can work out the other words.

11 **1836** M = 1, A = 8, S = 3, T = 6
12 **6481** T = 6, E = 4, A = 8, M = 1
13 **3814** S = 3, A = 8, M = 1, E = 4
14 **1446** M = 1, E = 4, T = 6
15 **SEAT** 3 = S, 4 = E, 8 = A, 6 = T
16 **dearest** 'E' does not appear twice in 'BROADEST'.
17 **beast** There is no 'T' in 'BECAUSE'.
18 **please** 'E' does not appear twice in 'PLANETS'.
19 **yearn** There is no 'Y' in 'BEARING'.
20 **eager** 'E' does not appear twice in 'STRANGER'.

Test 31: Mixed (page 32)

7 **905** D = 9, E = 0, N = 5
8 **@ $! %** T = @, R = $, A = %, P = T
9 **UQB** Y = U, A = Q, P = B
10 **x – = +** T = x, O = –, L = =, D = +
11 **marmalade** 'Marmalade' goes best as, like the others, it is associated with breakfast.
12 **tiger** 'Tiger' goes best as a tiger has the attributes listed; the others do not.
13 **collar** 'Collar' goes best as it is part of a garment like the listed words.
14–16 Category A contains words that are animals or mammals (**fox**)
Category B contains words to do with furniture (**cupboard, table**)
Category C contains words that are fish (**dogfish**)
Category D contains words that are fruit (**banana, grapes**)
17 **whole, part** 'Whole' is when something is entire or complete. A 'part' is opposite as it is incomplete or a fraction of a 'whole'.
18 **delicate, hardy** 'Delicate' means flimsy or weak, whereas 'hardy' is tough or resilient.
19 **believe, doubt** If you 'believe' in something or someone you trust them. If you 'doubt' something or someone you don't trust or believe in them.
20 **anxious, carefree** If you are 'anxious' you are worried. 'Carefree' means to have no worries.

Test 32: Mixed (page 33)

1. LEAP
2. LEMON
3. QUIET
4. SLEET
5. DIAL
6. CHARM
7. **post** postcard, postbox, postcode, postman
8. **sun** sunburn, sunglasses, sunset, sunshine
9. **child** childhood, childproof, childlike, childminder
10. **foot** footprint, footpath, footbridge, football
11. **N** 1 + 2 + 3 + 6 = 12. 12 = N
12. **M** 12 ÷ 2 = 6. 6 = M
13. **N** 6 × 2 = 12. 12 = N
14. **L** 6 − 3 = 3. 3 = L
15. **6** This is an alternating pattern. The first, third and fifth number increases by 3 each time. The second, fourth and sixth number is 1 every time.
16. **424** The numbers increase by 101.
17. **12** The numbers decrease by 3.
18. **D42** The letters are in a repeating pattern: DEFDEF. The numbers decrease by 7.
19. **3** The numbers are halved each time.
20. **17** The number added increases by 1 each time: +1, +2, +3, +4, +5

Test 33: Mixed (page 34)

1. **PJ** The first letter moves backwards one place. The second letter is in a repeating pattern: HHIIJJ.
2. **IR** The first letter (lower case) moves forward one place. The second letter moves backwards one place.
3. **E5** The letters are in a repeating pattern: EFGEFG. The numbers decrease by 1.
4. **DP** The first letter in each pair moves forwards two places. The second letter in each pair moves forward one place.
5. **GH** The first letter in each pair moves forward one place. The second letter moves forward two places.
6. **SB** The first letters are in a repeating pattern: SMSMSM. The second letters move backwards by one place.
7. **b** crib, book; stab, busy
8. **a** area, apple; gala, ask
9. **g** drag, gone; wing, glory
10. **t** cat, token; goat, tail
11. **harm** Bot**harm**ies were exhausted.
12. **iced** Mary thinks orange ju**iced** rinks are best.
13. **then** Pass **the n**etball to Natasha.
14. **team** The head teacher looked qui**te am**used.
15. **leaf** The bread was sta**le af**ter a few days.
16. **stench, smell** Both the words mean a stink or unpleasant aroma.
17. **join, connect** Both words mean to attach or link.
18. **bend, curve** Both words mean a turn or a twist.
19. **pen, pencil** Both of these are writing implements.
20. **need, require** Both these words mean to regard something as essential.

Test 34: Mixed (page 35)

1–5 Use grids as shown below to help work out the missing word.

1 WENT

1	2				3	4		1	2				3	4
P	A	W	N		R	U	L	E		W	E	S	T		D	E	N	T

2 DRAB

1		2			3	4		1		2			3	4
F	E	E	L		D	R	I	P		D	O	O	R		C	R	A	B

3 FAME

1	2				3	4		1	2				3	4
W	A	R	N		T	I	D	E		F	A	C	E		C	A	M	E

4 EACH

1			2	3	4		1			2	3	4
S	A	L	T		O	M	E	N		E	V	E	N		A	C	H	E

5 FLAT

	3	4		1	2			3	4		1	2
B	O	T	H		K	N	E	W		B	A	T	H		F	L	O	P

6. **bedrooms** A 'hotel' is where you spend a night. It therefore must have 'bedrooms'.
7. **ink** A 'pen' may have all these things but it is not a 'pen' without 'ink'.
8. **a nose** A 'nose' is the only integral part of a 'face'.
9. **long ears** 'Long ears' are an integral part of a rabbit.
10–15 The three glass containers are by the river. As green glass is the middle of the three, it must be C and brown glass next to it in B. Card is opposite to brown glass, so F. Card is between plastics and shoes. As green glass (C) is not opposite shoes, then plastics must be G and shoes E, leaving newspapers, which have not been mentioned, in A.

card F
shoes E
plastics G
green glass C
brown glass B
newspapers A

16 **sketch**
17 **fowl**
18 **quick**
19 **light**
20 **rule**

Test 35: Mixed (page 36)

1–3

P	I	T	C	H
A	■	O	■	O
T	■	K	■	N
H	■	E	■	E
S	U	N	N	Y

4–6

P	A	R	C	H
O	■	O	■	O
■	K	I	T	E	S
E	■	■	O	■	T
R	■	R	■	S

7 **present** To 'present' something means to hand over a gift as well as to display something.
8 **jam** 'Jam' is a sticky, sugary conserve as well as meaning to shove or force.
9 **quick** 'Quick' means clever and smart as well as speedy and swift.
10 **well** 'Well' means in good health, not ill and also a place dug into the ground where water is found.
11 **LIMB**
12 **BUY**
13 **PEAR**
14 **PARK**
15 **NM** Each letter moves backwards two places.
16 **Gt** The first letter moves forward one place. The second letter moves backwards two places.
17 **3SQ** The numbers increase by 1. Both letters move backwards one place.
18 **RT** Each letter moves forward four places.
19 **S5** The letters move forward one place. The numbers decrease by 2.
20 **IG** Each letter moves backwards four places.

Test 36: Mixed (page 37)

1 **S11** The letters are in a repeating pattern: SRSRSRSR. The numbers are in an alternating pattern. The first, third, fifth and seventh numbers increase by 2. The second, fourth, sixth and eighth numbers increase by 1.
2 **14** The numbers are in an alternating pattern. The first, third, fifth and seventh number increase by 1. The second, fourth, sixth and eighth number increase by 2.
3 **9** The numbers are in an alternating pattern. The first, third, fifth and seventh numbers go decrease 2. The second, fourth, sixth and eighth numbers decrease by 1.
4 **40** This is an alternating pattern. The numbers decrease by 8. The letters are in reverse alphabetical order.
5 **X9** This is an alternating pattern. The first, third, fifth and seventh letters move forward one place, while the numbers increase by 3. The second, fourth, sixth and eighth pair is always 2k.
6–9 Solve these questions by looking at the first set of three and working out how the first and last numbers have been used to arrive at the middle number. Apply this to the second set of three and see if it works. If it does, apply it to the last set.
6 **8** $6 - 3 = 3$ and $5 - 4 = 1$, so $9 - 1 = 8$
7 **1** $12 \div 3 = 4$ and $12 \div 6 = 2$, so $12 \div 12 = 1$
8 **10** $5 + 4 + 2 = 11$ and $3 + 7 + 2 = 12$, so $5 + 3 + 2 = 10$
9 **2** $(10 \div 2) - 1 = 4$ and $(6 \div 3) - 1 = 1$, so $(15 \div 5) - 1 = 2$
10 **CRAB** To get from the code to the word, move each letter backwards two places.
11 **WILL** To get from the code to the word, move each letter forwards two places.
12 **POLE** To get from the code to the word, move each letter forwards two places.
13 **POST** To get from the code to the word, move each letter forwards one place.
14 **LOOP** To get from the code to the word, move each letter backwards two places.
15 **FILE** To get from the code to the word, move each letter backwards one place.
16 **alive** 'Dead' means lifeless, so the opposite is 'alive' as this means full of life.
17 **expensive** 'Cheap' means inexpensive, so the opposite is 'expensive' which means costing a lot.
18 **release** 'Hold' means to keep captive, to retain, so the opposite is 'release' which means to set free or let go.
19 **sluggish** 'Brisk' is to be lively or energetic, so the opposite is 'sluggish' which means inactive or slow.
20 **patterned** 'Plain' is ordinary or basic, so the opposite is 'patterned' which means decorated.

Test 37: Mixed (page 38)

1–4 Two of the numbers begin with 1. This must be B. Three of the numbers have 37 in the middle. Therefore, 3 = E and 7 = A. Two of the numbers end in 5. This must be D. You can now identify all the letters.
1 **5793** D = 5, A = 7, R = 9, E = 3
2 **1379** B = 1, E = 3, A = 7, R = 9
3 **9375** R = 9, E = 3, A = 7, D = 5
4 **1375** B = 1, E = 3, A = 7, D = 5
5 **BREAD** 1 = B, 9 = R, 3 = E, 7 = A, 5 = D
6 **hooves, paws** A 'sheep has 'hooves' in the same way as a 'dog' has 'paws'.

7 **cricket, hockey** A 'bat' is used to play 'cricket' in the same way as a 'stick' is used to play 'hockey'.
8 **difficult, easy** 'Complicated' means 'difficult' in the same way as 'simple' means 'easy'.
9 **loose, tight** 'Slack' means 'loose' in the same way as 'taut' means 'tight'.
10 **hurl, toss** 'Throw' means 'hurl' in the same way as 'cast' means 'toss'.
11 **entrance, arrival** 'Exit' is the opposite of 'entrance' as 'departure' is the opposite of 'arrival'.
12–15 Category A contains words that are countries (**Spain, Norway**).
Category B contains words that are colours (**yellow, orange**).
Category D contains words that are items of clothing (**shirt, hat**).
Category A contains words that are modes of transport (**van, bus**).
16 **mend** 'Mend' means to put right or repair; similarly 'recover' means to become right.
17 **tender** 'Tender' is to be gentle and loving in the same way as 'caring'.
18 **value** 'Value' is merit or significance in the same way as 'worth'.
19 **hollow** 'Hollow' means there is nothing in the interior in the same way as 'empty'.
20 **ignorant** 'Ignorant' indicates a lack of knowledge in the same way as 'unaware'.

Test 38: Mixed (page 39)

1–5 Arrange the words in a grid to make it easier to put them in the correct alphabetical order.

1 **higher**

h	i	n	g	e		4th
h	i	g	h	e	r	3rd
h	e	l	l	o		2nd
h	a	r	d	e	r	1st
h	o	u	s	e		5th

2 **stork**

s	t	o	r	k	3rd
s	t	o	n	e	1st
s	t	o	r	y	5th
s	t	o	r	m	4th
s	t	o	o	l	2nd

3 **paths**

| p | a | t | r | o | l | | 4th |
| p | a | t | t | e | r | n | 5th |

p	a	t	h	o	s		2nd
p	a	t	h	s			3rd
p	a	t	c	h			1st

4 **front**

f	r	a	m	e		1st
f	r	i	n	g	e	2nd
f	r	o	w	n		5th
f	r	o	n	t		3rd
f	r	o	s	t		4th

5 **torch**

t	o	r	c	h	3rd
t	o	u	c	h	4th
t	e	a	c	h	1st
t	o	o	t	h	2nd
t	r	a	i	n	5th

6 **mauls**   7 **skate**
8 **throne**   9 **braid**
10 **snare**   11 **l** fan, seal
12 **y** ear, brainy
13 **n** sore, bend
14 **h** heat, thorn
15 **GN** The first letter moves backwards one place each time. The second letter is in a repeating pattern: LLMMNN.
16 **Z11** The letters are in a repeating pattern: ZYZYZY. The numbers increase by 2 each time.
17 **Gr** The first letters move forward by one place. The second letters move backwards by one place.
18 **JK** Each pair of letters moves forward in alphabetical order but the second, fourth and sixth pair are reversed.
19 **VI** The first letter moves forward one place whereas the second letter moves backwards one place.
20 **SL** The first letter moves forward two places. The second letter moves backwards one letter.

Test 39: Mixed (page 40)

1 **bizarre, weird**
2 **prize, value**
3 **near, by**
4 **precious, valuable**
5 **tatters, shreds**
6 **DATE**
7 **BOAT**

8 **CART**
9 **PAIN**
10 **E** 12 ÷ 6 = 2. 2 = E
11 **B** (12 − 10) x 5 = 10. 10 = B
12 **B** 5 x 2 = 10. 10 = B
13 **E** (6 x 2) − 10 = 2. 2 = E
14–15 **The Atlantic is one of the world's oceans. There are oceans in the world.**
The other three statements may or may not be true. You must reject them as they are not referred to in the information.
16 **WIG** & = W, * = I, / = G
17 **WIT** < = W, ! = I, ? = T
18 **KEEP** ~ = K, x = E, + = P
19 **ATOM** / = A, ^ = T, * = O, $ = M
20 **LOT** < = L, ; = O, > = T

Test 40: Mixed (page 41)

1–5 Use a grid to help you.

1	2	3	4	5	6	7	8	9	10
A	B	C	D	E	F	G	H	I	J

1 **HIDE**   2 **FEED**
3 **4935**   4 **31754**
5 **4516**
6 **plate**, **knife** Here is a knife to spread the jam on your toast.
7 **thunder**, **lightning** The flash of lightning lit up the night sky.
8 **seagulls**, **sheep** The sheepdog guided the flock of sheep down the hillside.
9 **newsagent**, **newspapers** As a family we recycle bottles, cans, cardboard and newspapers.
10 **car**, **man** A policeman helped the old man cross the road and carried his shopping bags for him.
11 **red**, **green** As the traffic lights turned to green, the cars started to move forwards.
12–15 From the information, you know that the beagle scored 10 (half marks), the Alsatian scored 16 (20 − 4), the dalmatian scored 15 (10 + 5) and the collie 18 (15 + 3).
12 **15**   13 **collie**
14 **10**   15 **dalmatian**
16 **pet, baby** The other words are ways of moving.
17 **slow, kind** The other words are to do with moving at speed.
18 **remove, carry** The other words are to do with putting a layer on something.
19 **frame, crayon** The other words are all forms of enclosure.
20 **rude, scowling** The other words are all to do with being sociable and kind.

Puzzle 1 (page 42)

Try each pair of letters against the two letters already in the bridge. Only one pair will link successfully. Cross them off as you go. The first pair to insert is '-EL' to make 'FEEL' and then 'EL-' must be matched with the next pair and so on.

LI		
FE		
EL		
SE		
AL	SO	RE
		IN
		TO
	NE	ST
		UN
		TO
		OK

Puzzle 2 (page 43)

In the first brick 'CAMP' can only be matched with 'FIRE' to make 'CAMPFIRE'. Both 'FIREWORK' and 'FIREPLACE' are possible, so work down both strands. 'PLACE' can make 'PLACEMENT' but then comes to a dead end afterwards, so retrace your steps and try again following 'FIREWORK' and repeat the process till you reach the bottom.
The other bricks work in exactly the same fashion.

CAMP
ROUND **FIRE**
WATER **WORK** PLACE
WHEEL SHOP **OUT** MAT
CHAIR FRONT SIDE **DOOR** TIN
TABLE WAYS **MAN** STOP
CLOTH **AGE** KIND
LESS HEARTED
ON

TURN
OVER NIP
HAND GROWN PER
SOME FULL UP FORM
HOW TIME LOAD ALL LESS
EVER SHARE RIGHT ROUND
GREEN HOLDER WING
HOUSE MIRROR
WIFE

Puzzle 3 (page 44)

All the possible pathways work and make sense except towards the end. With A, the second last instruction goes south instead of north taking Sarah away from home. With B, the last instruction cannot be fulfilled as it hits a wall. On the third last instruction (E2) with D, the route should have gone westwards towards home instead of entering a dead end. C is the only possible pathway.

Puzzle 4 (page 45)

Take the letters given and rearrange them to make words of three letters or more. For example 'OWE' can be made from the letters of 'FLOWER'. Here are some possible answers:
FLOWER: row, wore, lower, for, owe, wolf, owl
SPRING: pig, grin, sprig, rig, ring, grins, pin
LEAVES: veal, leave, ale, seal, slave, see
GARDEN: den, dare, anger, red, darn, range

Puzzle 5 (page 46)

On the grid, put in all the information you can, ticks as well as crosses. For example, put crosses on 5, 7 and 14 for Mia.
Nathan has yellow dice so tick his yellow box and put crosses in for red, blue and green. Rohan has blue dice so cross all the colours he does not have, as well as a tick for the blue dice. When you have got this far, you will find that Mia and Sita have three crosses for their colour dice. Mia must have red and Sita GREEN. Tick it and put crosses for red for the other children.
Rohan has not thrown 7 so cross that. You know that Sita must have 5 as she has the green dice. This leaves Nathan to have 7 and Rohan 14. Your grid is now complete.

	Red	Blue	Yellow	Green		5	7	12	14
Mia	✓	✗	✗	✗		✗	✗	✓	✗
Nathan	✗	✗	✓	✗		✗	✓	✗	✗
Rohan	✗	✓	✗	✗		✗	✗	✗	✓
Sita	✗	✗	✗	✓		✓	✗	✗	✗

Children	Colour of dice	Number of sixes
Mia	red	12
Nathan	yellow	7
Rohan	blue	14
Sita	green	5

Test 24: Mixed

Give the missing numbers and letters in the following sequences.

Example 2 4 6 8 10 <u>12</u>

1 3A4 4B5 5C6 6D7 7E8 ____
2 9 ____ 17 21 25 29
3 13 15 ____ 19 21 23
4 ____ 20H 25G 30G 35F 40F

Find the four-letter word hidden at the end of one word and the beginning of the next word. The order of the letters may not be changed.

Example The children had ba<u>ts and</u> balls. <u>sand</u>

5 The policeman's helmet fell over his eyes. _____
6 She gave me my favourite magazine. _____
7 We will miss our turn. _____
8 The twins are both in the show. _____
9 "Best foot forwards!" shouted the major. _____

Underline the two words, one from each group, which are closest in meaning.

Example (race, shop, <u>start</u>) (finish, <u>begin</u>, end)

10 (wood, camp, shoot) (tent, metal, fire)
11 (bus, train, chair) (school, sit, teach)
12 (pair, many, plenty) (single, two, none)
13 (note, diary, poem) (drawing, map, journal)
14 (path, road, pavement) (park, street, city)

Solve the problems by working out the letter codes. The alphabet has been written out to help you.

A B C D E F G H I J K L M N O P Q R S T U V W X Y Z

Example In a code, SECOND is written as UGEQPF.
How would you write THIRD? <u>VJKTF</u>

15 In a code, LAYER is written as MBZFS. What is LAND? _____
16 In a code, SLEEP is written as RKDDO. What is MINT? _____
17 In a code, PLAIN is written as RNCKP. What is NAIL? _____
18 In a code, GUESS is written as FTDRR. What is DESK? _____
19 In a code, THROW is written as UISPX. What is BALL? _____
20 In a code, FUDGE is written as DSBEC. What is GRID? _____

Time for a break! Go to Puzzle Page 44

Test 25: Mixed

Underline the two words, one from each group, which are most opposite in meaning.

Example (dawn, <u>early</u>, wake)   (<u>late</u>, stop, sunrise)

1. (nurse, divide, kind)   (sort, cruel, caring)
2. (most, more, least)   (less, lose, some)
3. (clean, misty, clear)   (dirty, spotless, shiny)
4. (speak, talk, answer)   (question, reply, whisper)

Find and underline the two words which need to change places for the sentence to make sense.

Example She went to <u>letter</u> the <u>write</u>.

5. Begin over your papers and turn.
6. There at over thirty children were the party.
7. The channels will not change television.
8. He watered the hose with a garden.
9. Edith burnt butter on her spread toast.
10. Sometimes I push my little swing on the sister.

Give the missing numbers and letters in the following sequences.

Example 5   21   8   17   11   13   <u>14</u>   9

11	6	30	7	___	8	20	9	15
12	11e	20y	13e	15y	___	10y	17e	5y
13	C	14	E	17	G	___	I	23
14	10	12	8	___	6	6	4	3
15	A9	X5	A7	X5	A5	X5	___	X5

Underline the two words which are made from the same letters.

Example TAP   PET   <u>TEA</u>   POT   <u>EAT</u>

16	PARTS	STARE	STRAP	RESTS	PRESS
17	STEEL	LEAST	TAUPE	LEAPT	PLATE
18	PROUD	SPOOL	LOOPS	DROOP	SOUPS
19	DEALER	READER	TREADS	LEADER	SPREAD
20	STEAL	LEAST	STOOL	LASTS	STALL

Test 26: Mixed

Test time: 0 — 5 — 10 minutes

Look at the first group of three words. The word in the middle has been made from the other two words. Complete the second group of three words in the same way, making a new word in the middle.

Example PAIN INTO TOOK   ALSO __SOON__ ONLY

1 KIND DROP ROPE   DEEP _____ LAYS
2 DRAG RAGE FINE   NEAT _____ CATS
3 WANT WIRE FIRE   FOOT _____ TOOL
4 LATE TEST STOW   MOON _____ CENT
5 PINE PEAT WHAT   STUN _____ FLOW

Underline one word in the brackets which is most opposite in meaning to the word in capitals.

Example WIDE (broad vague long <u>narrow</u> motorway)

6 SLOW (loose fast last sluggish late)
7 TRICKY (awkward clever difficult straightforward sly)
8 WRONG (correct faulty mistaken untrue unsure)
9 RARE (unusual front back smooth frequent)
10 IMMATURE (unripe childish young mature long)

Which one letter can be added to the front of all these words to make new words?

Example _c_ are _c_ at _c_ rate _c_ all

11 ___ each   ___ ouch   ___ ear   ___ high
12 ___ our   ___ ill   ___ earth ___ air
13 ___ mile   ___ tuck   ___ pill   ___ pin
14 ___ ice   ___ edge   ___ earn   ___ ate

Fill in the missing letters and numbers. The alphabet has been written out to help you.

A B C D E F G H I J K L M N O P Q R S T U V W X Y Z

Example AB is to CD as PQ is to __RS__.

15 BD is to CE as DF is to ____.
16 PO is to NM as LK is to ____.
17 Lm is to No as Pq is to ____.
18 QO is to PN as OM is to ____.
19 15QR is to 13RS as 11ST is to ____.
20 T22 is to U33 as V44 is to ____.

27

Test 27: Mixed

Underline the pair of words most opposite in meaning.

Example   cup, mug   coffee, milk   <u>hot, cold</u>

1. relaxed, strict   stone, rock   garden, house
2. pillow, bed   cushion, chair   soft, firm
3. luxury, riches   wealthy, poor   money, coins
4. stale, fresh   calm, peaceful   magical, fantastic

Complete the following sentences by selecting the most sensible word from each group of words given in the brackets. Underline the words selected.

Example   The (<u>children,</u> books, foxes) carried the (houses, <u>books,</u> steps) home from the (greengrocer, <u>library,</u> factory).

5. As the (elephants, lions, bears) waded across the (high street, river, mountain) they held their (passengers, trunks, suitcases) up high to keep them out of the water.
6. At four o'clock we cross the (lake, road, shop) outside school, looking left and (behind, wrong, right) because of the busy (traffic, police car, day).
7. John quickly (ran, tripped, crept) up the pitch dribbling the (bib, ball, secret) and scored the first (goal, test, baby) of the match.
8. As it is cold outside in the (fridge, playground, classroom), please (put on, take off, eat) your (shoes, coats, apples).
9. Clare, please sharpen your (pen, book, pencil) (over, under, beside) the (bed, mouse, bin).
10. I am already halfway through my very (exciting, eager, delicate) new (pillow, label, book) in the sixth (word, chapter, line).

If V = 10, W = 4, X = 3, Y = 1 and Z = 2, find the answer to the following calculations.

11. $\frac{V}{Z}$ = _____
12. (YZ) + W = _____
13. (XY) – Z = _____
14. VW = _____

Solve the problems by working out the letter codes. The alphabet has been written out to help you.

A B C D E F G H I J K L M N O P Q R S T U V W X Y Z

Example   In a code, SECOND is written as UGEQPF. Decode VJKTF.   <u>THIRD</u>

15. In a code, WEDGE is written as UCBEC. Decode UCCB.   _____
16. In a code, STERN is written as RSDQM. Decode EHQL.   _____
17. In a code, HARSH is written as JCTUJ. Decode JWTV.   _____
18. In a code, BIRCH is written as CJSDI. Decode GPVS.   _____
19. In a code, RIFLE is written as QHEKD. Decode KHED.   _____
20. In a code, BADGE is written as CBEHF. Decode CJSE.   _____

Test 28: Mixed

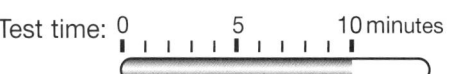

Test time: 0 5 10 minutes

Underline the two words which are made from the same letters.

Example   TAP   PET   <u>TEA</u>   POT   <u>EAT</u>

1   PERCH   CHURCH   PEACH   CHIRP   CHEAP
2   TOAST   STOAT   START   TASTE   ROAST
3   CARTS   SHARK   TRACE   STARK   CRATE
4   PRAISE   ASLEEP   STRIPE   PLEASE   SPITE
5   STRAW   WASPS   STATE   SPATE   TASTE

Choose two words, one from each set of brackets, to complete the sentence in the best way.

Example   Smile is to happiness as (drink, <u>tear</u>, shout) is to (whisper, laugh, <u>sorrow</u>).

6   Venison is to deer as (chops, beef, fish) is to (sheep, cow, chicken).
7   Television is to watch as (radio, ladder, chair) is to (talk, sound, listen).
8   Red is to pink as (black, colour, paint) is to (dark, grey, white).
9   Sunrise is to sunset as (cloudy, afternoon, dawn) is to (dusk, morning, breakfast).
10 Carrot is to vegetable as (cabbage, apple, lettuce) is to (pear, potato, fruit).
11 Kitchen is to cook as (bathroom, bedroom, playroom) is to (sleep, eat, drive).

Some girls were asked which books they had with them in their bags one afternoon.
Ann, Mira and Chloe had spelling books.
Davina and Ann had library books.
Beth had a photo album.
Mira and Chloe had Maths books.
They all had reading books except for Mira.

12   Who had a spelling book as well as a library book?   _____
13   Who did not have a Maths or a library book?   _____
14   Who had a reading book and a Maths book?   _____
15   How many books did Ann have?   _____

Solve the problems by working out the codes.

16   If the code for CATCH is LMNLO, what is the code for CHAT?   _____
17   If the code for BOOKS is ARRNT, what is the code for SOB?   _____
18   If the code for ACTOR is FBYBS, what is the code for ROTA?   _____
19   If the code for TRAIN is CZALP, what is the code for ART?   _____
20   If the code for PATCH is WZLTO, what is the code for PACT?   _____

Total

Test 29: Mixed

Find the letter which will end the first word and start the second word.

Example peac (h) ome

1 cra (___) oxes   2 gir (___) ast   3 dog (___) oup   4 bat (___) arp

Underline the word in each line that has its letters in alphabetical order.

5 fast   force   fixes   first   fusion
6 abacus   alert   accent   actual   agent
7 blood   blot   blame   blown   bloom
8 hinge   height   hippo   humus   hilly

If the letters of the alphabet are coded as A = 1, B = 2, C = 3 and so on, what words would these codes make?

9   10   1   4   5   _____
10 9   3   5   4   _____

Encode these words using the same code as above.

11 FADE _____   12 HEED _____

Read the statements and then underline two of the five options below that must be true given the information.

13–14 'Cars and vans are vehicles. All vehicles travel on the road.'
  Only vans travel on the road.
  Cars travel on roads.
  All vehicles are cars.
  Vans drive fast.
  Roads are for vehicles to travel on.

15–16 'Lions and tigers are related. They are all members of the cat family.'
  My cat is a lion.
  My cat is related to a lion.
  All cats are tigers.
  The cat family includes tigers.
  Lions eat tigers.

Give the missing numbers in the following sequences.

Example 2 4 6 8 10 _12_

17 3   4   ___ 9   13   18
18 7   ___ 15   19   23   27
19 16 18   20   ___ 24   26
20 20 18   16   14   ___ 10

Test 30: Mixed

Test time: 0 — 5 — 10 minutes

Find and underline the two words which need to change places for the sentence to make sense.

Example She went to <u>letter</u> the <u>write</u>.

1 Is the bottom of the garden there at a shed.
2 The road stopped at the bottom of the bus.
3 Jake for eggs and bacon had breakfast.
4 Go please to bed now.
5 The trees fell off the leaves.
6 She in her fork and knife put the dishwasher.

Underline two words, one from each group, that go together to form a new word. The word in the first group always comes first.

Example (hand, <u>green</u>, for) (light, <u>house</u>, sure)

7 (quarter, whole, half) (turn, size, some)
8 (bent, side, up) (cash, fall, set)
9 (for, in, by) (spot, deed, date)
10 (wind, black, screw) (wood, screen, barn)

Here are the number codes for four words. Match the right code to the right word.

MAST   SAME   TEAM   MEET
1446   1836   3814   6481

11 MAST _____   12 TEAM _____
13 SAME _____   14 MEET _____

Using the same code, decode:

15 3486 _____

Underline the one word which **cannot be made** from the letters of the word in capital letters.

Example STATIONERY stone tyres ration <u>nation</u> noisy

16 BROADEST strode trade breast toads dearest
17 BECAUSE   sauce   beast cease   case   cubes
18 PLANETS   stale   plant steal   please staple
19 BEARING   yearn   grain brine   bring brain
20 STRANGER grate   range stare   great eager

Test 31: Mixed

Test time: 0 – 5 – 10 minutes

Fill in the crosswords so that all the given words are included. You have been given one letter as a clue in each crossword.

1–3 NOTED PLANK SENDS WARTS LEAVE

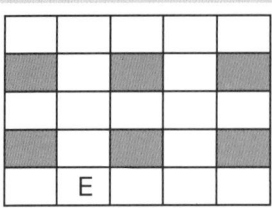

4–6 BRAND BARBS DREAD SHRED RANGE

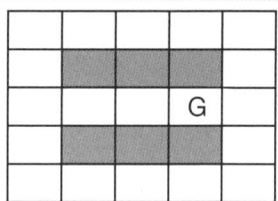

Solve the problems by working out the codes.

7 If 8059 stands for MEND, what is DEN? _____
8 If % ! $ @ stands for PART, what is TRAP? _____
9 If BZQU stands for PLAY, what is YAP? _____
10 If + − = × stands for DOLT, what is TOLD? _____

Underline the word in the brackets which goes best with the words given outside the brackets.

Example word, paragraph, sentence (pen, cap, <u>letter</u>, top, stop)

11 cereal, toast, milk (curry, marmalade, gravy, soup, beetroot)
12 tail, stripes, fangs (zebra, wolf, tiger, snail, hippo)
13 sleeve, buttonhole, pocket (jeans, cloth, scarf, collar, fashion)

Look at these groups of words.

A	B	C	D
elephant	wardrobe	shark	melon
cat	chair	cod	apple
sheep	bed	salmon	peach

Choose the correct group for each of the words below. Write in the letter.

14–16 dogfish ____ cupboard ____ banana ____ table ____ fox ____ grapes ____

Underline the two words, one from each group, which are the most opposite in meaning.

Example (dawn, <u>early</u>, wake) (<u>late</u>, stop, sunrise)

17 (spare, whole, eager) (complete, part, quick)
18 (apart, instant, delicate) (hardy, course, dainty)
19 (believe, touch, pull) (find, take, doubt)
20 (open, anxious, free) (carefree, concerned, careful)

32

Total

TEST 32: Mixed

Rearrange the letters in capitals to make another word. The new word has something to do with the first two words or phrases.

Example spot soil SAINT __STAIN__

1. jump hop PEAL _____
2. fruit citrus MELON _____
3. silent peaceful QUITE _____
4. snowy icy rain STEEL _____
5. disk clock face LAID _____
6. enchant dazzle MARCH _____

Find a word that can be put in front of each of the following words to make new, compound words.

Example cast fall ward pour __down__

7. card box code man _____
8. burn glasses set shine _____
9. hood proof like minder _____
10. print path bridge ball _____

If J = 1, K = 2, L = 3, M = 6 and N = 12, find the answer to the following. Write your answer as a letter.

11. J + K + L + M = ___
12. $\dfrac{N}{K}$ = ___
13. MK = ___
14. M − L = ___

Give the missing numbers and letters in the following sequences.

Example 2 4 6 8 10 __12__

15. 3 1 ___ 1 9 1
16. 121 222 323 ___ 525 626
17. 18 15 ___ 9 6 3
18. ___ E35 F28 D21 E14 F7
19. 96 48 24 12 6 ___
20. 7 8 10 13 ___ 22

Time for a break! Go to Puzzle Page 45 ▶

33

Total _____

Test 33: Mixed

Give the missing letters and numbers in the following sequences.
The alphabet has been written out to help you.

A B C D E F G H I J K L M N O P Q R S T U V W X Y Z

Example	CQ	DP	EQ	FP	GQ	<u>HP</u>
1	TH	SH	RI	QI	____	OJ
2	jT	kS	____	mQ	nP	oO
3	E8	F7	G6	____	F4	G3
4	BO	____	FQ	HR	JS	LT
5	____	HJ	IL	JN	KP	LR
6	SF	ME	SD	MC	____	MA

Find the letter which will complete both pairs of words, ending the first word and starting the second. The same letter must be used for both sets of words.

Example   mea (t) able   fi (t) ub

7 cri (___) ook   sta (___) usy
8 are (___) pple   gal (___) sk
9 dra (___) one   win (___) lory
10 ca (___) oken   goa (___) ail

Find the four-letter word hidden at the end of one word and the beginning of the next word. The order of the letters may not be changed.

Example   The children had bat<u>s and</u> balls.   ___sand___

11 Both armies were exhausted.   _____
12 Mary thinks orange juice drinks are best.   _____
13 Pass the netball to Natasha.   _____
14 The head teacher looked quite amused.   _____
15 The bread was stale after a few days.   _____

Underline the two words in each line which are most similar in type or meaning.

Example   <u>dear</u>   pleasant   poor   extravagant   <u>expensive</u>

16	stench	smell	drain	flower	soap
17	join	ear	win	connect	lose
18	push	bend	stretch	curve	shrink
19	compass	rubber	pen	ruler	pencil
20	need	enjoy	bake	dislike	require

Test 34: Mixed

Test time: 0 – 5 – 10 minutes

Look at the first group of three words. The word in the middle has been made from the other two words. Complete the second group of three words in the same way, making a new word in the middle.

Example   PA<u>IN</u>   <u>IN</u>TO   T<u>OO</u>K   ALSO   <u>SOON</u>   ONLY

1	PAWN	PALE	RULE	WEST	_____	DENT
2	FEEL	FLIP	DRIP	DOOR	_____	CRAB
3	WARN	WADE	TIDE	FACE	_____	CAME
4	SALT	SOME	OMEN	EVEN	_____	ACHE
5	BOTH	KNOT	KNEW	BATH	_____	FLOP

Choose the word or phrase that makes each sentence true.

Example   A LIBRARY always has (posters, a carpet, <u>books</u>, DVDs, stairs).

6   A HOTEL always has (restaurants, elevators, bedrooms, air conditioning, a garden).
7   A PEN always has (a lid, a case, ink, a cartridge, a book).
8   A FACE always has (a smile, freckles, glasses, a nose, make up).
9   A RABBIT always has (carrots, a hutch, an owner, long ears, spots).

Here is a plan of a recycling area. From the information below, work out what is recycled in each bin.
Here is a list of the things that are recycled:

```
_____
              River
                              White Glass
   (A)     (B)     (C)     (D)
                              Cans
   (E)     (F)     (G)     (H)
```

Card is between plastics and shoes and opposite to brown glass.
The glass containers are next to each other by the river.
Green glass is the middle glass container and is not opposite the shoes' bin.

10–15   card _____   shoes _____   plastics _____
green glass _____   brown glass _____   newspapers _____

Find a word that is similar to the word in capital letters and that rhymes with the second word.

Example   CABLE   tyre   <u>wire</u>

16	DRAW	fetch	_____	17	CHICKENS	towel	_____
18	FAST	sick	_____	19	PALE	spite	_____
20	LAW	tool	_____				

35

Total

TEST 35: Mixed

Test time: 0 5 10 minutes

Fill in the crosswords so that all the given words are included. You have been given one letter as a clue in each crossword.

1–3

SUNNY PATHS
HONEY PITCH
TOKEN

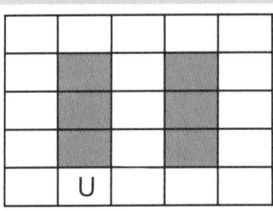

4–6

PARCH KITES
POKER ROTOR
HOSTS

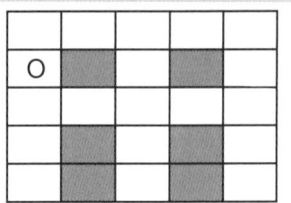

Underline the one word in the brackets which will go equally well with both the pairs of words outside the brackets.

Example rush, attack   cost, fee   (price, hasten, strike, <u>charge</u>, money)

7 give, award   show, exhibit   (welcome, card, tell, present, gift)
8 jelly, preserves   push, squeeze   (butter, jam, stick, stuff, pack)
9 intelligent, sharp   fast, rapid   (swift, prompt, clever, blunt, quick)
10 fine, healthy   hole, water   (fit, drain, pond, well, right)

Remove one letter from the word in capital letters to leave a new word. The meaning of the new word is given in the clue.

Example AUNT   an insect   ___ANT___

11 CLIMB   leg   _____
12 BUOY   purchase   _____
13 PEARL   fruit   _____
14 SPARK   public garden   _____

Fill in the missing letters and numbers. The alphabet has been written out to help you.
A B C D E F G H I J K L M N O P Q R S T U V W X Y Z

Example AB is to CD as PQ is to _RS_.

15 TS is to RQ as PO is to ____.
16 Dw is to Ev as Fu is to ____.
17 3XV is to 4WU as 2TR is to ____.
18 FH is to JL as NP is to ____.
19 P11 is to Q9 as R7 is to ____.
20 NL is to JH as MK is to ____.

Test 36: Mixed

Give the missing numbers and letters in the following sequences.

Example   5   21   8   17   11   13   <u>14</u>   9

1	S5	R3	S7	R4	S9	R5	___	R6
2	7	12	8	___	9	16	10	18
3	12	11	10	10	8	___	6	8
4	___	z	32	y	24	x	16	w
5	V3	2k	W6	2k	___	2k	Y12	2k

Find the missing number by using the two numbers outside the brackets in the same way as the other sets of numbers.

Example   2 [8] 4   3 [18] 6   5 [<u>25</u>] 5

6   6 [3] 3   5 [1] 4   9 [__] 1
7   12 [4] 3   12 [2] 6   12 [__] 12
8   5 [11] 4   3 [12] 7   5 [__] 3
9   10 [4] 2   6 [1] 3   15 [__] 5

Solve the problems by working out the letter codes. The alphabet has been written out to help you.

A B C D E F G H I J K L M N O P Q R S T U V W X Y Z

Example   In a code, SECOND is written as UGEQPF. Decode VJKTF.   <u>THIRD</u>

10   In a code, SPACE is written as URCEG. Decode ETCD.   _____
11   In a code, STEEP is written as QRCCN. Decode UGJJ.   _____
12   In a code, SLOPE is written as QJMNC. Decode NMJC.   _____
13   In a code, PHONE is written as OGNMD. Decode ONRS.   _____
14   In a code, PLANE is written as RNCPG. Decode NQQR.   _____
15   In a code, DRAIN is written as ESBJO. Decode GJMF.   _____

Underline one word in the brackets which is most opposite in meaning to the word in capitals.

Example   WIDE   (broad   vague   long   <u>narrow</u>   motorway)

16   DEAD   (lifeless   alive   working   gone   arrive)
17   CHEAP   (chick   low   high   expensive   money)
18   HOLD   (twist   hug   release   contain   grip)
19   BRISK   (active   breezy   sluggish   snail   quick)
20   PLAIN   (modest   clear   colour   patterned   frank)

Test 37: Mixed

Test time: 0 5 10 minutes

Here are four number codes: 5793   1375   9375   1379.
Match them to the four words below.

1 DARE _____
2 BEAR _____
3 READ _____
4 BEAD _____

Using the same code, decode:

5 19375 _____

Complete the following sentence in the best way by choosing one word from each set of brackets.

Example Tall is to (tree, <u>short</u>, colour) as narrow is to (thin, white, <u>wide</u>).

6 Sheep is to (lamb, wool, hooves) as dog is to (kennel, paws, bark).
7 Bat is to (cricket, tennis, rugby) as stick is to (football, hockey, swimming).
8 Complicated is to (soft, difficult, intelligent) as simple is to (nasty, tricky, easy).
9 Slack is to (hard, loose, strict) as taut is to (rope, tight, tied).
10 Throw is to (catch, fetch, hurl) as cast is to (toss, play, count).
11 Exit is to (hole, entrance, door) as departure is to (arrival, airport, customs).

12–15 Look at these groups of words.

A	B	C	D
India	red	socks	train
England	black	shorts	car
America	green	trousers	bicycle

Choose the correct group for each of the words below. Write in the letter.

Spain _____   shirt _____   yellow _____
orange _____   hat   _____   van   _____
Norway _____   bus   _____

Underline the word in brackets closest in meaning to the word in capitals.

Example UNHAPPY (unkind   death   laughter   <u>sad</u>   friendly)

16 RECOVER (bend   send   lend   mend   tend)
17 CARING   (mother   kiss   sore   tender   temper)
18 WORTH   (bill   time   value   add   money)
19 EMPTY   (filled   hollow   heavy   bursting flooded)
20 UNAWARE (ignorant aware   beware   mind   awful)

TEST 38: Mixed

In each line underline the word which would come in the middle if the words were arranged in alphabetical order. The alphabet has been written out to help you.

A B C D E F G H I J K L M N O P Q R S T U V W X Y Z

1	hinge	higher	hello	harder	house
2	stork	stone	story	storm	stool
3	patrol	pattern	pathos	paths	patch
4	frame	fringe	frown	front	frost
5	torch	touch	teach	tooth	train

Underline the one word which **can be made** from the letters of the word in capital letters.

Example	CHAMPION	camping	notch	peach	cramp	<u>chimp</u>
6	FAMOUSLY	mouse	yours	flame	flour	mauls
7	BASKET	token	bathe	skate	tasty	fable
8	ANOTHER	thorny	train	hotter	throne	notes
9	BIRTHDAY	youth	braid	bathe	death	hardly
10	GARDENS	snare	green	snore	drain	sender

Move one letter from the first word and add it to the second word to make two new words.

Example	hunt	sip	_hut_	_snip_
11	flan	sea	_____	_____
12	year	brain	_____	_____
13	snore	bed	_____	_____
14	heath	torn	_____	_____

Give the missing letters and numbers in the following sequences. The alphabet has been written out to help you.

A B C D E F G H I J K L M N O P Q R S T U V W X Y Z

Example	CQ	DP	EQ	FP	GQ	<u>HP</u>
15	KL	JL	IM	HM	____	FN
16	Z3	Y5	Z7	Y9	____	Y13
17	____	Hq	Ip	Jo	Kn	Lm
18	FG	IH	____	ML	NO	QP
19	UJ	____	WH	XG	YF	ZE
20	MO	ON	QM	____	UK	WJ

39

Test 39: Mixed

Test time: 0 — 5 — 10 minutes

Underline the pair of words most similar in meaning.

Example   come, go   <u>roam, wander</u>   fear, fare

1   bizarre, weird   perfect, misshapen   green, grass
2   appreciate, ignore   prize, value   effort, laziness
3   out, in   beside, underneath   near, by
4   precious, valuable   priceless, worthless   costly, cheap
5   rags, riches   tatters, shreds   scraps, cloth

Change the first word into the last word by changing one letter at a time and making a new, different word in the middle.

Example   CASE   __CASH__   LASH

6   DOTE   _____   DARE
7   COAT   _____   BEAT
8   CAST   _____   CURT
9   RAIN   _____   PAIR

If A = 12, B = 10, C = 6, D = 5 and E = 2, find the answers to the following calculations. Give the answer to each calculation as a letter.

10   $\frac{A}{C}$ =   ____   11   (A − B) × D =   ____
12   D × E =   ____   13   (C × E) − B =   ____

Read the statements and then underline two of the five options that must be true given the information.

14–15   'The Atlantic is an ocean. Oceans surround the lands of the world.'

There are four oceans in the world.
The Atlantic is one of the world's oceans.
Oceans are large bodies of water.
There are oceans in the world.
Whales live in the Atlantic Ocean.

Solve the problems by working out the codes.

16   If & * \ / stands for WING, & * / stands for _____.
17   If < % ! ? stands for WAIT, < ! ? stands for _____.
18   If + x x ~ stands for PEEK, ~ x x + stands for _____.
19   If $ * / ^ stands for MOAT, / ^ * $ stands for _____.
20   If > ; ; < stands for TOOL, < ; > stands for _____.

40

Total

Test 40: Mixed

If the letters of the alphabet are coded as A = 1, B = 2, C = 3 and so on, what words would these codes make?

1. 8945 _____
2. 6554 _____

Encode these words using the same code as above.

3. DICE _____
4. CAGED _____
5. DEAF _____

Change one word so that the sentence makes sense. Underline the word you are taking out and write your new word on the line.

Example I waited in line to buy a <u>book</u> to see the film.   _ticket_

6. Here is a plate to spread the jam on your toast. _____
7. The flash of thunder lit up the night sky. _____
8. The sheepdog guided the flock of seagulls down the hillside. _____
9. As a family we recycle bottles, cans, cardboard and newsagent. _____
10. A policeman helped the old car cross the road and carried his shopping bags for him. _____
11. As the traffic lights turned to red, the cars started to move forwards. _____

Four dogs were judged at a dog show out of a total of twenty marks.

The Beagle scored half marks.
The Alsatian only lost 4 marks out of 20.
The Dalmatian got 5 more marks than the Beagle but 3 less than the Collie.

12. How many marks did the Dalmatian receive? _____
13. Which dog won the competition? _____
14. How many marks did the Beagle receive? _____
15. Which dog did better than the Beagle, but not as well as the Alsatian? _____

Underline the two words which are the odd ones out in the following groups of words.

Example black <u>king</u> purple green <u>house</u>

16. run   pet   crawl   baby   walk
17. quick   rapid   fast   slow   kind
18. remove   blanket   cover   spread   carry
19. cage   frame   coop   crayon   pen
20. friendly   rude   cheerful scowling pleasant

Time for a break! Go to Puzzle Page 46

Total

Puzzle 1

Help to build a bridge across the crocodile infested river. Use the word boxes at the bottom of the page to make words that link together – the last two letters of the first word make the first two letters of the next word.

The first word has been placed for you.

| LI |
| FE |

AL	SE
ST	NE
RE	UN
TO	IN
EL	OK
TO	SO

Puzzle 2

Start at the top of the pile of bricks and, working through the layers, make new words by combining two words, one from one layer and the other from the layer below it.

You must go down each time, not sideways.

Here is an example:

BLACK
OUT | BERRY
DOOR

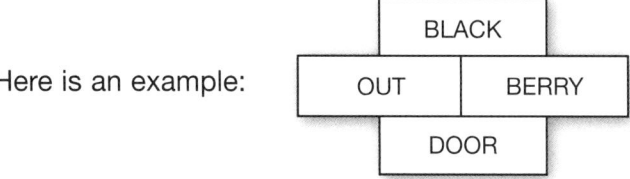

Both BLACKOUT and BLACKBERRY are new words, but only

OUTDOOR makes sense as the next word.

Now try these. Be careful, there is only one path through!

CAMP
ROUND | FIRE
WATER | WORK | PLACE
HEEL | SHOP | OUT | MAT
CHAIR | FRONT | SIDE | DOOR | TIN
TABLE | WAYS | MAN | STOP
CLOTH | AGE | KIND
LESS | HEARTED
ON

TURN
OVER | NIP
HAND | GROWN | PER
SOME | FULL | UP | FORM
HOW | TIME | LOAD | ALL | LESS
EVER | SHARE | RIGHT | ROUND
GREEN | HOLDER | WING
HOUSE | MIRROR
WIFE

Puzzle 3

Sarah is tired and wants to go home.

There are several routes that will take her home, but her mother wants her to use a specific one. She has given Sarah written instructions to follow.

Unfortunately, Sarah's older brother has placed three other sets of instructions in Sarah's backpack. Which is the correct set of instructions to take her back home?

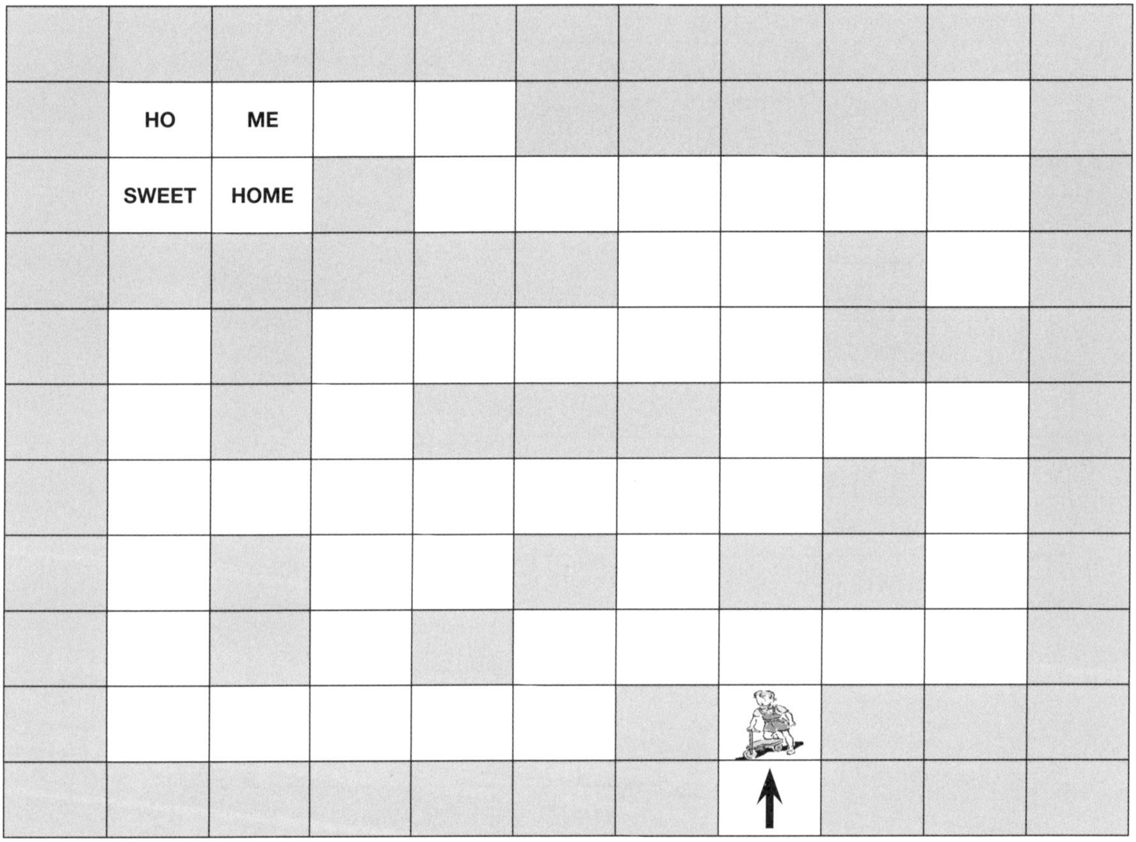

The letters show the compass directions (north, south, east, west). The numbers show the number of squares Sarah should travel (for example, N1 means go north, 1 square).

Here are the four sets of instructions:

A	B	C	D
N1	N1	N1	N1
W1	W2	E2	W1
N2	S1	N3	N2
W3	W4	W2	E1
N2	N3	N3	N4
E4	E2	W3	E2
S2	N2	N1	N1
W4	W1	W2	W1

Puzzle 4

In the centre of each flower is a word. Write a word on each of the petals that can be made using the letters of the centre word. You may only use each letter once. Each word must be three or more letters long.

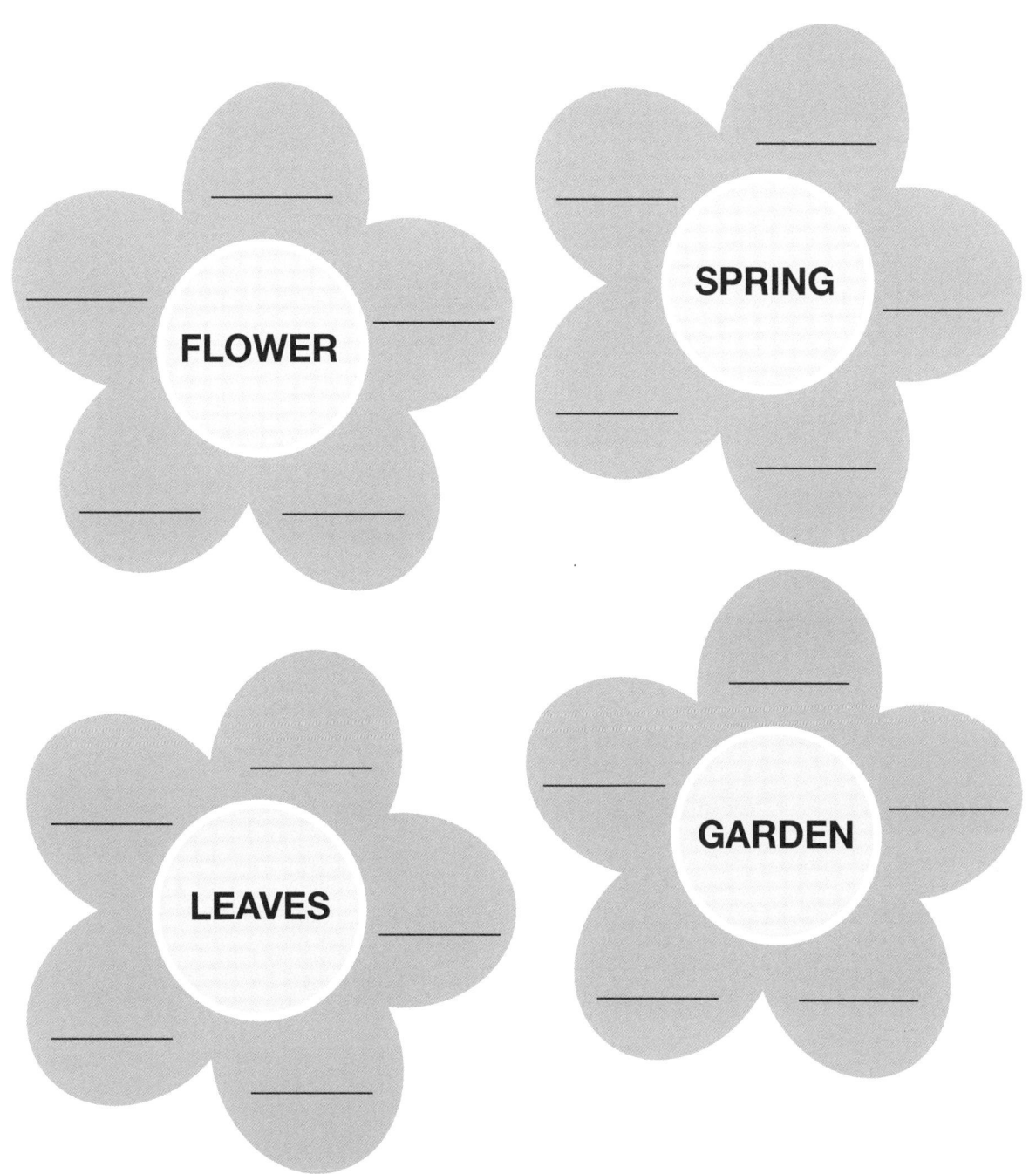

Puzzle 5

Mia, Nathan, Rohan and Sita played a game of dice. Each of them had a pair of different coloured dice – red, blue, yellow or green. The idea of the game was to throw as many sixes as they could in 20 throws. They ended up throwing 5, 7, 12 and 14 sixes.

Using the grid and clues below, work out which colour dice each child had and how many sixes he or she threw.

The first clue has been done for you.

	Colour of dice				Number of sixes			
	Red	Blue	Yellow	Green	5	7	12	14
Mia			X	X			✔	
Nathan								
Rohan								
Sita								

Clues:

1. Mia scored 12 sixes. Mia does not have yellow or green dice.
2. Nathan has yellow dice.
3. Rohan has blue dice but has not thrown 7 sixes.
4. The child with the green dice has the lowest score.

Your grid should now be complete. Fill in the table below to show the number of sixes each child scored and their dice colour.

Children	Colour of dice	Number of sixes
Mia		
Nathan		
Rohan		
Sita		

Progress Grid

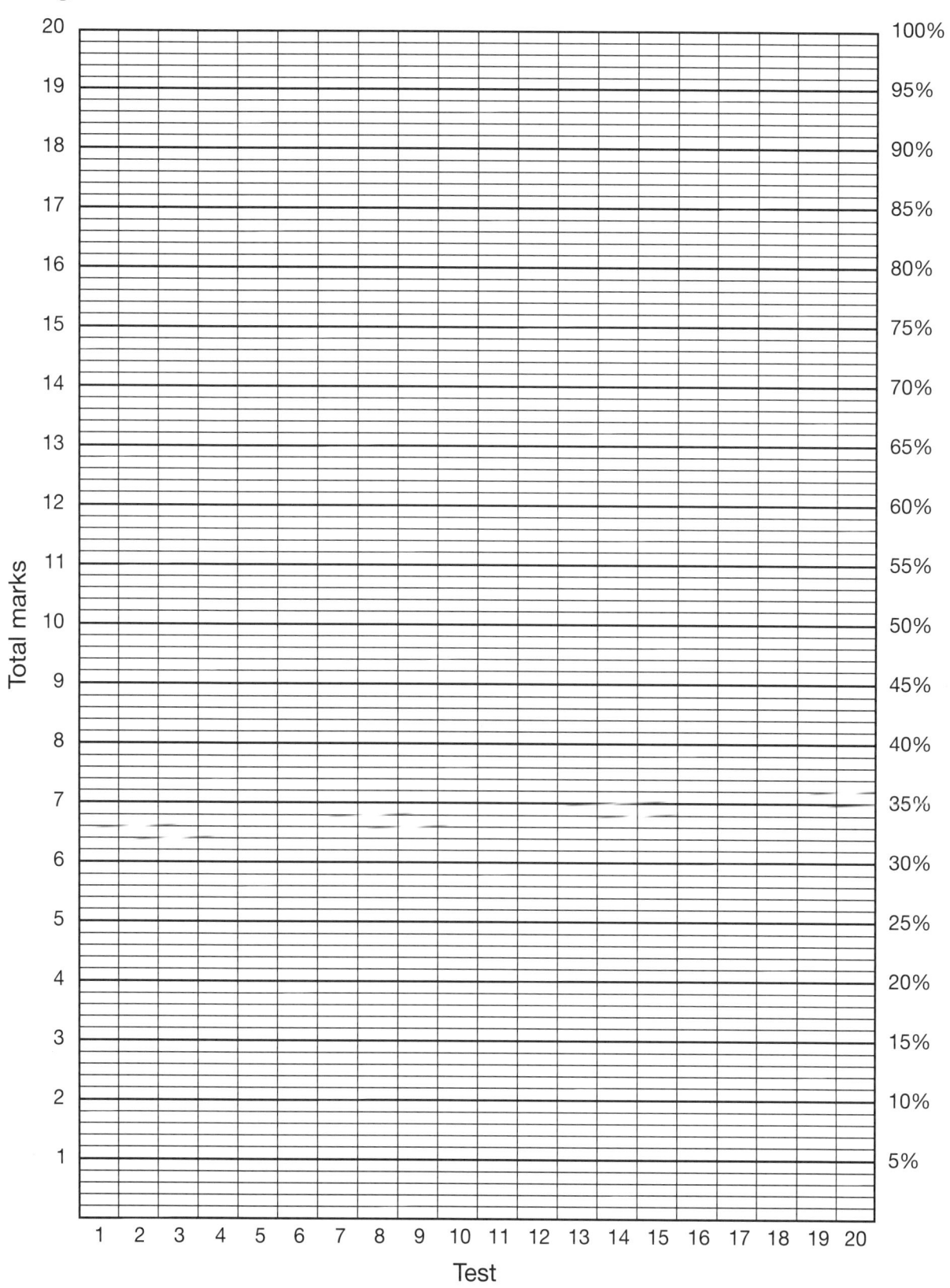

Progress Grid

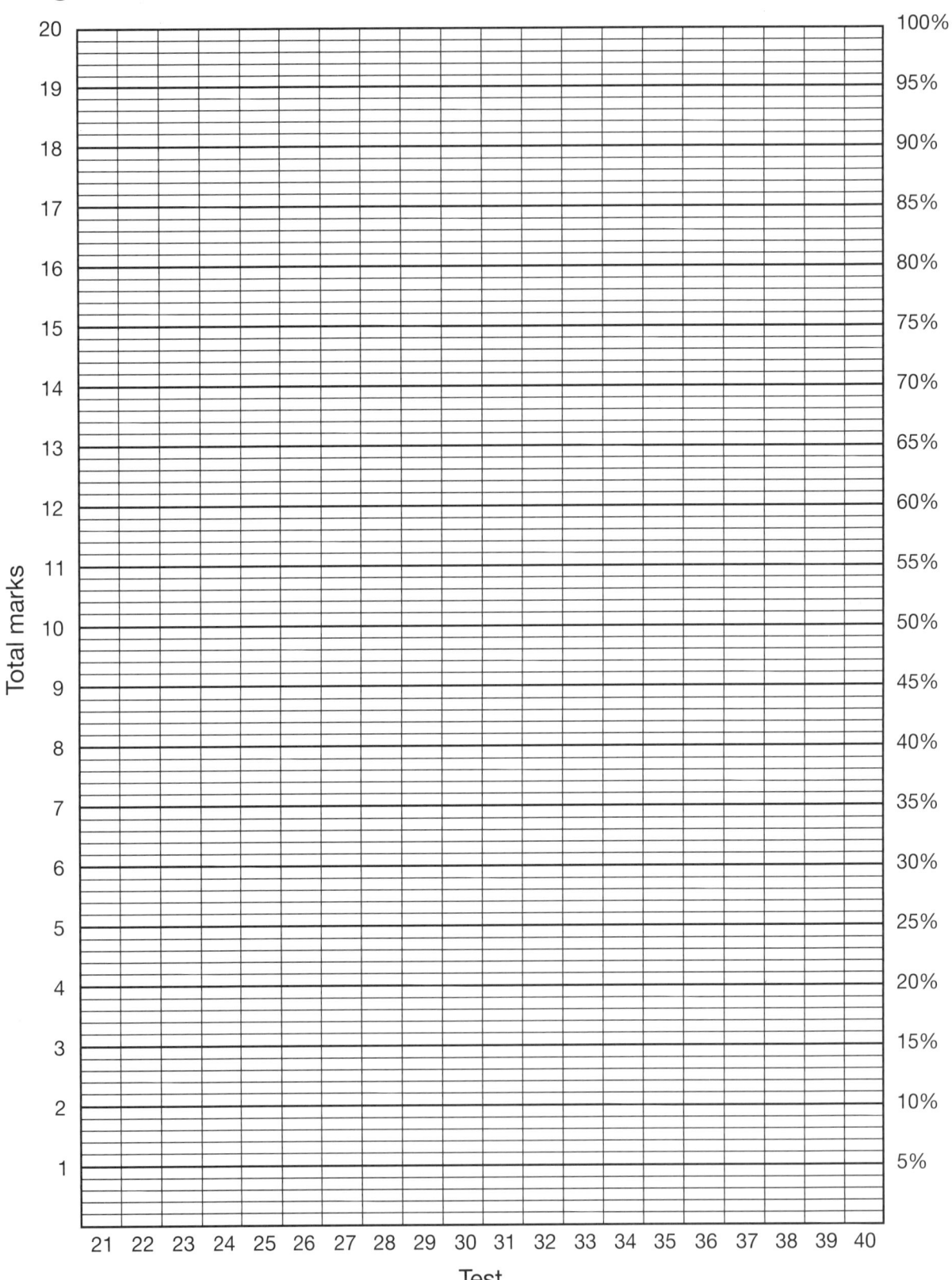